THE CLASSIC SUNBEAM

Chris McGovern

MERCIAN

Mercian Manuals Ltd
353 Kenilworth Road
Balsall Common
Coventry, CV7 7DL
www. mercianmanuals.co.uk

ISBN 978 1 903088 44 9

Contents

Acknowledgements *6*
Introduction *7*
1. The Designer and the Design *13*
2. Development and Production *25*
3. The Hybrids *76*
4. Competition *94*
5. Special Tuning *141*
6. What to Look for when Buying an Alpine *171*
7. Clubs and Spares *178*
Appendices
I. Road Test Reports *197*
II. Identification of Engine and Chassis Numbers *228*
III. Production Figures *230*
IV. Performance Figures *231*
V. Comparison of Performance
Figures Obtained in Road Tests *231*
VI. Body Dimensions, Weights and Capacities *238*
VII. Technical Specifications *243*
Index *253*

Acknowledgements

A great number of people contributed to this book, many of whom had to recall events which happened over twenty years ago, and it is to them that I would like to express my thanks: namely (in alphabetical order) Alec Caine, Gerry Ealson, Charles Eyre-Maunsell, Peter French, Mike Green, Peter Harper, Clive Harrington, Justin Harrington, Kenneth Howes, Mr. Lea Major, John Melvin, Peter Proctor, Bernard Unett, Mark Woodfine, and not forgetting those mentioned in the chapters concerning special tuning and the clubs.

I would also like to thank *Motor* and *Autocar* magazines for allowing me to publish their road test reports (all copyrights for these are held by the respective magazine); Acton Library and the National Motor Museum, Beaulieu for allowing me to search through their least-used files; and Rolls-Royce Ltd. for some superb production-line photographs. My special thanks go to Talbot (UK) Ltd. who supplied the majority of the illustrations reproduced in this book: these have not been credited individually. They also allowed me full access to various departments, enabling me to delve into the memories of those employees who worked for the Rootes Group in the 1960s. The co-operation and hospitality shown to me by these people, and by the company as a whole, was truly exceptional.

My greatest appreciation goes to my wife and son, who have had to cope with my monomania, and last but by no means least to Margaret Gilson of Spennymoor, Co Durham, and my father John, who between them managed to read, understand and then convert my scribble into typescript – by no means an easy task.

Finally, if I have forgotten to mention you, I hope you will forgive me! I hope you will find sufficient compensation in the book itself.

Introduction

Just how far back is it necessary to go to introduce a book about the Rootes Group's Sunbeam Alpine? So little has been written about such a great firm that in my opinion we have to go back to the beginning, to see how the Rootes Group developed from a small cycle shop in Kent to one of the biggest motor manufacturing companies in Britain.

William Rootes, the father of William Edward, later Lord Rootes, was not a wealthy man, but a small-time business man who ran a bicycle shop at Hawkhurst in Kent. Believing that both his sons, William and Reginald, should start their career with a good education, he insisted that they were sent to Cranbrook School. By the time they were ready to leave school, at 16, he had prospered, adding a motor agency to his bicycle shop, but neither son decided to join the family business, each preferring to go his own way. William Edward started his career as a penny an hour pupil at Singer Motors Ltd., little knowing that he would eventually own this company. During the 1914–18 War he served as a lieutenant in the R.N.V.R. and in 1917 he was given a special demobilization in order to pioneer a new development for that time – the establishment of a plant at Maidstone to enable aero engines to be repaired instead of being scrapped. The war ended before this was fully operative. He then contacted his brother Reginald, who by this time had a promising career as a civil servant at the Admiralty, and talked him into joining him in partnership in order to re-establish the car sales firm of Rootes Ltd.

7

The Rootes family's first cycle shop, at Hawkhurst, Kent.

In 1919 Reginald decided to join his brother at Maidstone, where you could say they started to build an empire. Reginald was a great administrator while William Edward was the salesman, showing an uncanny ability for assessing future trends in public taste. By 1926 they had acquired offices and showrooms in the heart of London's West End, at Devonshire House. Within a matter of months they had acquired other branches in various parts of the country and become the largest motor distributing company in Europe. As they prospered, many well known and old established firms in the motor industry began to feel the impact of economic recession. But while some companies closed down, the brothers accepted the challenge. With ideas of how to reshape some of these companies to meet the demands of the age of volume-production, they acquired an interest in the Hillman Car Co., followed shortly by a similar interest in Humber Ltd., which also included the Commer commercial vehicle concern. These three companies were failing fast, due to outdated plant and production methods, and gave the brothers a chance to put their ideas into reality.

The first Rootes car: the 1931 Hillman Wizard. (National Motor Museum, Beaulieu)

In 1931 the Hillman Wizard was launched as a new car for world markets. Although it met with only limited success they were not deterred, and it did give them time to unfold their ideas and to straighten out the firms they had acquired. By 1932 the Rootes Group was taking shape and they launched another car, the Hillman Minx, which turned out to be an immediate success. Their ideas had paid off, and the companies had been saved. Little did they know that the Minx name was to be used time and time again over the next four decades and has now become a classic name in motoring history.

The success of the Rootes Group was due to rationalization of production, and soon the time came to expand. They acquired Karrier Motors in 1935, control of Clemont Talbot in 1937, then British Light Steel Pressings, and by 1938 they had gained the Sunbeam Motor Co. They had in fact been supporting Sunbeams for a good many years prior to this.

1932 Hillman Minx: the first of the mass-produced Rootes cars. The name was to live on for a good number of years. (National Motor Museum, Beaulieu)

Many people have said that when the Rootes Group acquired these companies, the cars they produced were not, and should not be called Hillman, Humber, Talbot or Sunbeam. But these companies had been building dated cars on dated machines and were in urgent need of rationalization and, indeed, some form of integration. Apart from this, the brothers made sure that the identities of the marques were not submerged and this policy was continued until the Chrysler take-over in 1967. The luxurious Humbers, the sporting Sunbeams and the quality Hillmans all retained their distinctive personality. All the Rootes Group cars had quality and were built to last. Compare them with other contemporary marques of the same price range and tell me who comes out on top! By 1939 the Rootes Group were firmly established as one of Britain's 'Big Six' car manufacturers.

The first car to bear the name of Alpine: a George Hartwell conversion of the Sunbeam Talbot 90.

With the outbreak of the Second World War, the Rootes factories were turned over to the manufacture of military vehicles, but that is another story.

The post war reorganization saw yet another challenge for the Rootes brothers, the redevelopment of Britain's world trade. They played a leading part in organizing the motor industry's exports, and also established Britain's first assembly plants in Australia and other key market areas.

In 1950, as Chairman of the Society of Motor Manufacturers and Traders, William Rootes played the major role in organizing the first ever British Motor Show in the U.S.A. Held in New York the show netted over three million dollars' worth of exports. Trade with the U.S.A. began to escalate and in the six years from 1951 to 1956 it netted no less than 169 million dollars' worth. From 1957 to 1962 this figure had increased to over 303 million dollars.

In 1959 William Rootes was created a Baron and became Lord Rootes of Ramsbury. That year, the country saw the introduction not only of a new Lord, but of a new car, the Sunbeam Alpine.

The Sunbeam name would always be associated with sporting cars.

1

The Designer and the Design

Few motorists know who designed the cars they own and drive, and surprisingly few road test reports provide this information. There again, few cars are designed with so much style as to date all competitors immediately on release. The Alpine has proved an exception on all three counts and I suspect motoring magazines realized this and gave the designer the publicity he deserved.

Kenneth Howes, C.Eng., M.I.Mech.E. F.S.I.A.D. (Chartered Engineer, Member of the Institution of Mechanical Engineers and Fellow of the Society of Industrial Artists and Designers) was born in 1924 at Chippenham, Wiltshire, a pleasant stone-built market town, where he lived for a number of years, and attended the local school. He moved on to a school in Gloucester and eventually to Swindon College where he studied engineering.

Kenneth's career started only a few months after his 16th birthday when he was accepted as a student engineer in the Great Western Railway's main locomotive workshops at Swindon. It was not long before he realized what his ambition was. He had been reading and hearing about a designer called Raymond Loewry and was fascinated by the designs he was producing. He became determined then that one day he would work for Loewry and nothing was going to stop him from fulfilling his aim.

A man of many talents, Kenneth Howes could turn his hand to designing anything from ashtrays to motor cars that are still too futuristic to be put into production. (Kenneth Howes)

In 1945, when he was 21, he transferred to the materials testing and research laboratory. His thirst for knowledge was incredible and within six months he had gained a position in the drawing and design office where he began to build up quite a reputation. It didn't take him long to become recognized as a designer with potential and, in particular, with the ability to predict future trends.

In 1948 Raymond Loewry decided to open a London office and began looking for an Englishman to join his team. The Council of Industrial

Design, then at Petty France, London, put forward Kenneth Howe's name as a potential candidate. Kenneth recalls how, at the age of 24, he was asked to attend an interview with a view to joining Loewry's rather exclusive team: 'Right out of the blue, I received a telegram asking me to visit Raymond Loewry's London office for an interview. I could hardly believe it, and had no idea at that time that a London office was being opened. It was just a remarkable coincidence.' Raymond Loewry was then considered to be the leader in industrial design, having probably done more for the profession than anyone else. To be part of such a team was considered quite an experience and a great privilege.

Kenneth Howes was about to attend an interview which, if successful, would completely change his life. He selected his best drawings and photographs and went to Loewry's office. The interview took its course. He was asked what salary he wanted; he told them. The interview ended with no mention of whether he would even be considered for the job. This played on Kenneth's mind: with so many people being interviewed, had he over-estimated his value? He was convinced that he had let the chance of a lifetime slip through his fingers, and that the job had been lost because he had asked for too much money.

One of Howes' first designs after he joined the Loewry design team: a 9-inch room heater, designed in 1949 and selected for a touring exhibition in the U.S.A. (Kenneth Howes)

The next day, in a desperate attempt to save the situation, he sent a telegram to Loewry's office. It was short and to the point – 'Prepared to accept any reasonable salary offer, signed Howes' – obviously meaning he would accept less than he had previously stated. You can imagine his surprise when he received a telegram in reply offering even more and asking when he could start.

Kenneth Howes has always been a futuristic designer and no doubt Loewry saw his potential in the drawings and photographs he submitted at the interview. The general public were first made aware of Kenneth's talents on 26th October 1949, when at the age of 25 he wrote an article for *The Motor* magazine, expressing his opinions on probable trends in car design, 20 years hence.

'Within the next 20 years we can expect many revolutionary changes in car design. Whilst the most striking and obvious changes will be in the external appearance, an important selling factor, there is little doubt that the substitution of the gas-turbine for the piston type engine will prove equally significant. More exacting demands from the female element will inevitably result in drastic changes of interior design. Car designers will concentrate more on the unity of individual components so that they may achieve a more integral and functional whole.

'Naturally, the automobile gas-turbine will have many advantages over the piston type engine. It will be lighter, whilst giving the same power output, and simplicity of design, with few moving parts, will make for simpler maintenance. It will be easy to start, acceleration will be considerably improved, and there will be complete freedom from vibration. In cold weather there will not be the worry of cracked cylinder blocks, as unlike the majority of to-day's engines, the turbine will be air cooled.

'The gas turbine will be placed in the rear of the car, and requiring less height than the present-day engine, will enable the back of the car to be swept down to almost a point in side elevation allowing the designer greater scope for improved body design with a view to reducing the wind resistance. Tail shape is of very great importance in this respect. There is little point in streamlining the front of the car if the rear remains stunted and boxy. Neglect of this nature will defeat any attempt to reduce wind resistance. It is well known that the teardrop shape is ideal for achieving the least wind resistance, and it has been used in modified forms on cars attempting land speed records.

'A smooth under-tray completely encasing the bottom of the car will effectively reduce wind resistance, and at the same time seal the underside from dirt. Compartments suitable for luggage, spare wheel, tools etc. will take up the space which in to-day's cars is occupied by the engine. The front of the car will have a much cleaner appearance, as ornate chromium-plated radiator grilles and other forms of air intake will become completely superfluous. Rear engined cars will take in air from two streamlined air ducts placed, one on each side, at the rear of the car.

'Aluminium alloys may be expected gradually to supersede steel for both chassis and body construction, giving a valuable weight reduction. Serious consideration may also be given to the use of plastic materials for body construction. As long ago as 1941, the Ford Motor Company produced an all plastic car body with panelling having an impact strength ten times greater than the usual pressed steel, yet at the same time giving a weight reduction of one-third.

'Even bumpers and hub caps may become plastic, thereby making interesting colour changes possible, as under present conditions application of finish to these units is practically confined to chromium plate. Bumpers will become a more integral part of the car, being built into it rather than on to it, and will be connected to oil-cushioned shock absorbers.

'Window area will increase considerably, already Studebaker cars have made a bold move in this direction. A large percentage of highway accidents can be attributed to poor visibility from the driver's seat, and it is certain that the front window corner posts will be moved back, giving drivers an unrestricted view. It is probable that the roofing and glass windows will be replaced by a transparent plastic shell or blister of the type now used in many aircraft, having automatically controlled blinds to shield passengers from the glare of the sun.

'This development awaits the production of a suitable form of transparent plastic having the necessary resistance to abrasion. The problem could be overcome by giving the plastic some form of case hardening, and the shell could be reinforced with a light aluminium alloy structure to afford protection in the event of the car rolling completely over.

'Another cause of road accidents is the careless use of the present day hinged-type door, especially on the offside of the car. These will probably be replaced by a form of light, flush fitting door which, when swung out slightly, will slide, easily and silently, along the side of the car. Four doors will be replaced by two larger doors, and at the same time, maximum body strength will be maintained.

'Automobile design is in the melting pot, and it is obvious that many designers are drawing their inspiration from recent developments in aircraft design. One thing is certain: the car will obtain its beauty from purity in shape, relying less and less on bits and pieces of chrome trappings idly and often ostentatiously placed here and there on the body. Chromium plating and all unnecessary ornamentation will undoubtedly take back seat.

'Headlights, the designer's headache, often and inevitably giving the front of a car a grotesquely human appearance, are due for special attention. Shutters may hide them when they are not in use, and it is even conceivable that their size may be reduced by sinking the light source farther into the body of the car and using a lens system. This would, however, prove relatively expensive, although the improved appearance might justify the additional expenditure. An alternative approach to the same problem might be to merge the headlights into the actual car, the method used for landing lights in aircraft.

'Experiments have already been carried out to prevent dazzling by the headlights of oncoming cars. The system used entails the installation of polarized windscreens and headlights. If the plane of polarization of the windscreen is at a different angle to the plane of polarization of the headlights, the normal glare of the oncoming headlights is reduced to a gentle glow, although the visual effect for the driver of the oncoming car is not impaired in any way.

'In addition to certain safety features previously mentioned, it is likely that manufacturers will produce leather or plastic covered crash pads, to be affixed to instrument panels and the tops of front seats, alleviating the danger of cracked heads in the event of quick stops. Instrument panels will also be simplified, the present day untidy collection of instruments being supplanted by a neat and compact row of coloured indicator lights. Speedometers will be higher, to ensure minimum eye deflection. A complete re-design of the steering wheels and columns is probable and desirable. These may be made to move forward, in the event of a head-on crash, by means of an entirely new principle and there will be less likelihood of crushed ribs for drivers.

'The car has a very promising future before it; but we must beware of the element who seek ostentatious luxury and who would have our cars become hotels on wheels, complete with folding beds, television sets and built-in cocktail bars. A car is first and foremost a vehicle, a means of conveyance, and our aim must be to achieve perfection in this field before we seek to make a mobile home out of an automobile.'

I wonder how many members of the general public dismissed Kenneth Howes as some sort of eccentric with a vivid imagination, never thinking that any of these changes would take place. But he proved them wrong: most of his forecasts came true long before the twenty years were up, due in no small part to his own efforts. He himself was quite surprised at the impact the article made. Parts of it were published in other magazines and newspapers throughout the world and he was to see later

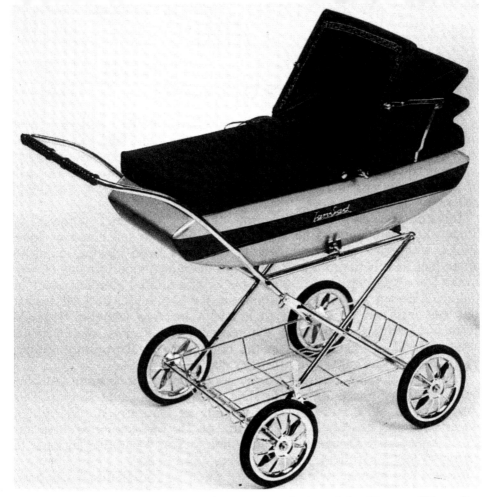

A scaled-down version of a baby carriage designed by Howes. When first introduced, this design increased sales by over 100 per cent and was copied all over the world. (Kenneth Howes)

copies of it in design studios he visited in the States in the early 1950s, not to mention the copy he found in the design studios of the Rootes Group when he joined them.

There is no doubt that the biggest stepping stone in Kenneth Howes' career was when he joined the Loewry Organization. He ended up as assistant to the chief designer and had a hand in designing cars, duplicating machines, clocks, electric cookers, bathroom fittings and a number of household essentials. In 1952 he transferred to the New York office of the Loewry Organization and later to Loewry's own design studios of the Studebaker Motor Company at South Bend, Indiana.

Howes left the Loewry organization at the beginning of 1955 and was then appointed head of a design studio at the Ford Motor Company in Detroit, which provided him with a valuable insight into highly geared efficiency methods, and the application of colour and study of texture on a vast scale. He worked on a wide range of automobile designs – new production models, facelifts for existing models, and both exterior and interior design. These were mainly futuristic, advanced designs, intended not for production but to develop ideas for possible future use. He says of the time he was there: 'There was always something new, something different – fascinating work.'

Towards the end of 1956, Bob Bourke, the chief designer at Studebaker, who used to be Howes' boss, wrote to tell him that John Panks, a director of Rootes Motors Inc., had been making enquiries about him. It is believed that Bourke was instrumental in bringing Howes to the Rootes Group. At the same time he was offered a professorship in industrial design at a major university in the U.S.A. He decided against this and returned to England to attend a meeting with Sir Reginald Rootes, Geoffry Rootes (later the second Lord Rootes) and Bernard Winter (head of engineering) in the boardroom at Devonshire House, Piccadilly. He was engaged by them at that meeting.

After the meeting Bernard Winter took him to his London club for lunch and gave him a general briefing on the situation at Rootes. This was followed by a more detailed briefing at Coventry on the design department and his role in that department. He was appointed Assistant Chief Appearance Designer, second in line to Ted White, the engineer in charge of the department, with Ted Green third in line.

Rootes' top management had wanted a new sports car that would have international appeal, believing that there was a ready market waiting for the right car. Unfortunately Jeff Crompton, Rootes' designer at the time, had made up a quarter scale model of a design he had in mind, but it was not acceptable. It was for this reason that Kenneth Howes was put completely in charge of the Alpine project which he was to carry through from the quarter scale model to the full size mock up.

He says, 'It was an exciting design opportunity; perhaps it was because of a sense of urgency – of limited time available – that caused the work to proceed very rapidly.' He had no preconceived ideas about what the car should look like. As he explained, although he made a few preliminary sketches, the design really evolved three-dimensionally on the quarter scale model. His aim was a body shape which would gain its effect from purity of sculptural form, and not from superfluous decoration.

It all started with what is called a 'buck', a box-like form crudely resembling the basic shape of a car which is screwed into place on a large squared baseboard. When Howes first joined Rootes they were using Plasticine for all the modelling, but he soon persuaded them to switch to the type of clay they used in American design studios. This clay is heated in special thermostatically controlled ovens to turn it into a plastic

Howes' original ¼-scale clay model for the new Sunbeam, incorporating a recessed wing on one side (facing camera) and a plain, flat wing on the other (not seen). The Rootes management opted for the flat wing and the design was accepted and put into production without any alterations. (Kenneth Howes)

workable state. The clay is built up around the wooden 'buck' and then cut and shaped with specially developed tools. It is a gradual process which takes a great deal of patience and imagination, the various surfaces continually being added to or cut away. Rootes wanted a car that would change the shapes of sports cars to come. They wanted a prestige model to market at a low price. Howes had already become internationally renowned for his futuristic designs; and he was now in the process of designing the car they wanted, a pace setter.

Time was pacing by, and the clay model was taking shape. One line was modified at a time, that change putting other areas out of balance, which had to be adjusted in turn. This process continued until a balanced design was achieved. It's true that almost anyone can design a car, but to achieve something that is both practical and different is another matter. It's a problem that can defeat even the best of designers, or so it would seem from the number of 'look alike' cars produced today. I asked Kenneth Howes how he set about designing the Alpine, and he told me, 'Personally I find that much of design is an intuitive process. I knew that I wanted a sports car with clean lines, a fast looking car with a good aerodynamic shape.'

The quarter scale model was taken to M.I.R.A. where the correctness of the body shape was verified by the wind tunnel tests. It was then scaled up to produce a full size wooden mock-up. When the seating buck

The wooden mock-up of the full scale design, showing the curved dashboard similar to that of the M.G.A. Howes had this removed as soon as he saw it: he immediately sat inside the mock-up and designed a new dashboard from plasticine. (Kenneth Howes)

first came into the design studios from the workshop, it had a double roll over the instrument panel (see photograph). Howes wasn't keen on this as he felt that it did not blend in with the rest of the body shape. While the project engineers got to work building the full scale wooden mock-up, he asked for another open seating buck to be made available.

He promptly sat down in this and modelled out of clay the version that eventually appeared on the production Alpines.

The mock-up was completed and painted a bold red, later given the name of Carnival red and used on production models. It was then placed on an electrically operated viewing turntable in the design studio, for its inspection by top management. Bearing in mind that this was the first time they had seen the design, you can imagine the atmosphere in the studio. In walked Lord Rootes, Sir Reginald Rootes, Bernard Winter and a few others. They mumbled amongst themselves, not letting their impressions be seen or overheard, when all of a sudden Johnny Johnson – the Alpine's project engineer at that time – overheard Sir Reginald say, 'Howes has done a good job.' Members of the Rootes family very rarely gave any sort of praise to anyone, and to hear one of them say that was an achievement in itself. The design had been accepted, exactly as it was. There were to be no objections, no modifications, no alterations.

Kenneth Howes with the first hand-built prototype. The car was originally going to be called the Sunbeam Sabre. (Kenneth Howes)

At the end of December 1957, work began on the first prototypes. At this stage the design had no name and was known by the number RAS 436. At one point the name 'Sabre' was applied to the door of the wooden mock up, the script lettering being cut out of aluminium to simulate chrome. In the end, Roote's management decided that they should re-introduce the name Alpine, and so the car was christened 'The Sunbeam Alpine'.

What of Kenneth Howes today? After he had completed the Alpine project, he decided that he did not want to specialize in car design, preferring instead the challenge of solving product design problems, with a particular emphasis on safety and improving the appearance of everyday objects. In recent years he developed a strange fascination for abstract art and has now turned his hand to drawing a cartoon strip for a newspaper. Called 'Ricky and Robin', the strip was described by a Canadian magazine: 'Little Ricky is a largely anthropomorphous character with a space suit and a permanent grin; Robin is a rather rigid bird who wears a nightcap at all hours. They streak about in space in a sleek ship called Starfish.'

When once asked to define his purpose, Kenneth Howes replied 'The job of an industrial designer is to interpret the function of useful things in terms of appeal to the eye, to endow them with beauty of form and colour, and to create in the consumer the desire to possess.'

The public's response to the Alpine upon its release was sure proof that he had fulfilled this purpose. His ambition is to see a Sunbeam Alpine on display in the Museum of Modern Art in New York. As you can see, the Alpine is something he feels very strongly about.

2
Development
and Production

Like most other sports cars of the same era, including Triumphs, M.G.s, and Sprites, the Alpine was based on components volume produced for saloon cars. The chassis/floorpan of the Alpine originated from the Hillman Husky while most of the mechanical parts came from the Sunbeam Rapier. The Rapier's parts caused no problems for the project engineers: they had been more than adequately proven in the numerous rally and track events the car had competed in. But the Husky's chassis/floorpan was a different matter altogether, and caused a great amount of concern prior to production. It was an ideal design for the Husky, but when it was used to produce the convertible it lost an enormous amount of stability as it relied on the roof of the saloon to stop it from flexing. In this respect, the choice of this floorpan was certainly not a wise one.

By the middle of 1958 the project team were ready to have the first metal prototypes built. This gave the already overworked Rootes engineers another project to complete 'last week'. To ease the burden it was decided to call in outside help from a local firm, Abbey Panel and Sheet Metal Co. Ltd., to assist them in making some of the body panels. Since the panels had to be hand-made, this saved a considerable amount of time. This procedure is not unusual for the larger car manufacturers, as they have a very limited number of their own engineers available, who also have to handle the updating of all the current models already in production. In fact, this method normally works out cheaper in the long run, as it saves employing staff who would not normally be needed.

The pressure of work being carried out by all the Rootes employees, who at that time were working flat out to fulfil the orders on the order books, played a major role in the management's decision to sub-contract Alpine production entirely. Talks had already taken place with Bristol Siddeley Engines Ltd., who at that time were in the process of laying off workers due to a reorganization programme, with a view to reopening their Parkside works which had been standing empty for some time, and using it for the Alpine's production. Parkside was one of the oldest factories of the former Armstrong Siddeley car manufacturers and many people were overjoyed at the prospect of the Alpine bringing it back to life. Rootes knew that the extra high quality of the finished products produced by Armstrong workers would be in keeping with their policy.

The first prototype, known as RAS 1 (RAS standing for Rootes

After the internal layout had been sorted out, the first prototype, RAS 1, was allocated the registration number WDU 427. This photo shows Howes' redesigned dashboard.

Armstrong Siddeley), was registered and allocated the number WDU 427. This car was little more than a demonstration model for the project team to work on, to enable them look into the problems they might come up against in future production and to add final refinements. This was quickly followed by two further prototypes RAS 2 and RAS 3, allocated registration numbers WDU 808 and WDU 807 respectively.

RAS 2 was a right-hand-drive vehicle, fitted with wire wheels, and RAS 3 a left-hand-drive vehicle fitted with standard pressed steel wheels. Although playing a slightly more active role than RAS 1, these cars were never used for serious testing, but merely acted as guinea pigs for the RAS 1 refinements and for testing out the engine which was going to be used in production. The engine was basically a Rapier unit that had been uprated by fitting an aluminium cylinder head, designed by Ted Leigh of the Rootes engine development department.

After using RAS 1 to RAS 3 as a basis for production talks, a further eight prototypes were delivered to the engineers to enable the main

The first prototype shown here with the prototype soft top. The production models did not have the rear quarter lights, which impaired visibility quite considerably.

The hood was stowed away behind three hinged compartments, to maintain the smooth lines of Howes' design.

testing programme to commence. These were allocated registration numbers XRW 301 to XRW 308. Various locations had been chosen, mainly in Scotland, London and France, and the vehicles were given the final touches to make them suitable for road testing. This consisted of removing all the badges, and painting the cars dull grey and dull off white, then leaving them out in the dirtiest location at the factory to allow them to gather as much grime as possible. Apparently they worked on the assumption that nobody looked at a dirty car and the drivers were therefore unlikely to be asked embarrassing questions from inquisitive members of the public (and press).

The team of test drivers which Rootes had gathered together to work on the Alpine project carried the official titles of 'Road Development Engineers' but were better known around the factory as the 'set 'em alight boys'! It was always considered a privilege to be selected for any of the Sunbeam projects and this one was something special. Many considered them to be the best of their profession. One such man was

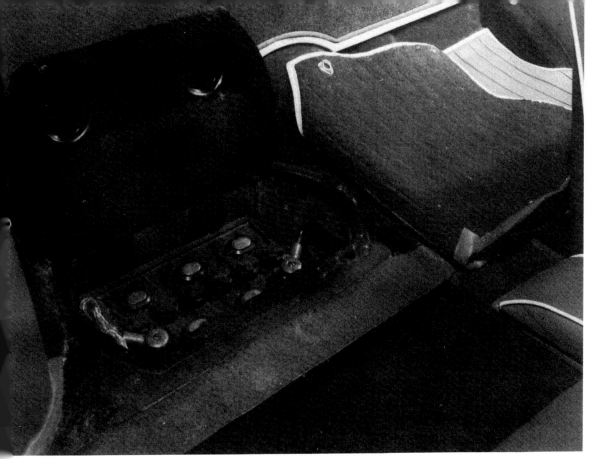

To save cluttering up the engine compartment, the battery was placed behind the driver's seat, under what can only jokingly be classed as the rear seat.

Bernard Unett, who summed them up as 'An incredibly closely knit team which would turn their hands to anything, the epitome of the cars.' They built up such a reputation that even today, those that have not since retired, still work together as development engineers.

The team was headed by Don Tarbun with Bernard Unett as his assistant, and consisted of Peter Coleman, Dennis Walden, Arthur Hadden, Bill Hillier, Maurice Sperling and Ray Elliot. Peter Coleman was unfortunately reallocated to another post within the Rootes Group early in the team's life, and was replaced by Brian Bateman.

The 'set 'em alight boys', so called because of the antics they got up to, were to carry out the serious testing of the Alpine on all types of surfaces and locations throughout the car's production life, sometimes having to drive in relays to keep the cars moving 24 hours a day just to trace any faults which might occur over long distances.

Before any long distance work was considered, it was necessary to take the vehicles to the testing ground to test body stability over rough

There was very little room for anyone to sit in the back. The rear seat had really to be considered as an extra parcel shelf, to compensate for the lack of space in the boot.

ground. Bernard recalls the first trials. 'It was frightening. As you know, the hoods (soft tops) were held by bolts about 2 inches long; these were just pulled out of their sockets: it was amazing, one minute the hood was there and the next it wasn't. I tell you, you didn't know what was going to fall off next. Needless to say we sat down and found out why it was happening.' This turned out to be the fault of the floorpan/chassis of the Hillman Husky, as described above. It was just not suitable for use on a convertible, but by this time it was too late to change it. With little more than 9 months to go before the scheduled release to the press, it was simply a matter of having to find a method of stopping the body flexing without disrupting the production time table. They knew why it was happening almost immediately, but arranging for a quick solution took a bit longer. Placing a large crossmember under the floorpan would have helped to eliminate the body flexing to an acceptable level, but unlike other companies, Rootes were not prepared to accept this – even though people had become accustomed to being told it was one of the hazards

The lockable arm rest compartment between the two front seats. Later versions were hinged at the rear, rather than at the side as on the early Series 1 shown here.

you had to take when buying a sports car. Thicker and thicker crossmembers were made and tried until the most suitable was found. This eliminated flexing to such a degree that almost all the motoring journalists who later test drove the Alpine commented on it, and expressed how surprised they were.

By eliminating this problem in this way, extra weight had been added to the original design, weight which nobody wanted and which no doubt interfered with the final performance figures. But, as I have been told time and time again, Rootes did not set out to produce the fastest car on the market. They wanted a prestige vehicle, offering all the luxuries and comforts of the most expensive vehicle then on offer. Yet, by keeping the price in the under £1,000 bracket, they aimed to outdate the models produced by their competitors by 10 years (or so the advertisements claimed), forcing them into the situation of having to think again.

All the prototypes were fitted with these crossmembers and returned to the testing ground. Once it had been established that all flexing was

One of the pre-production models is prepared at the secret hide-away in London — the base from which the cars were sent out under test in heavy traffic conditions. (Rolls-Royce Ltd.)

eliminated, the cars were gently run in at a constant 90 mph (gently they said!) before they were sent to their respective locations for testing. Three cars went to Scotland, three to France and two to London.

The two which went to London used Armstrong's West London factory as a base and from there they were taken into Central London each day for eight hours of driving. Eight hours of constant traffic jams, considered to be the worst in Britain – this was supposed to age a vehicle far quicker than any other method known. It places an incredible amount of stress on most of the working parts. Due to all the stopping and starting it is also a quick method of finding any potential overheating problems. This was a subject the designers had always worried about. The initial wooden mock up had been fitted with an egg crate type grille (grilles of the same design were later to be used on the Harringtons and Tiger Mk. II's) but they had found it necessary to replace this with the horizontal bar type grille used in production. They were afraid that even

Alec Caine (left) and Norman Garrad (right) with two of the prototype Alpines on test in the south of France. (Alec Caine)

The test cars were expected to do an average of 10,000 miles every two weeks. This was a sure way of discovering any potential faults. (Alec Caine)

Whilst under test, the cars were allowed to become as dirty as possible. The badges shown in this photo were removed, to hinder identification. (Rolls-Royce Ltd.)

this would not be sufficient, and sure enough, after only a short spell of the traffic-jam treatment the water temperature rose to boiling point. This gave Haddon and Tarbun something to work on. They changed the matrix of the radiator from steel to copper and continued their testing, to find that the overheating had been cured. They promptly reported their findings to Alec Caine who had been appointed the Alpine's project engineer (replacing Johnny Johnson who had been the project engineer since the start and whose expertise was now required on other projects). Lord Rootes, who was with Alec at the time, overheard the conversation and said sarcastically 'That will be cheaper of course', smiled and left the office.

While the testing continued most of the taller drivers complained of lack of leg room in their regular daily reports, but no other faults had been found. As the initial tests were scheduled to last two weeks, Alec set about trying to find those extra few inches of leg room. The only way to achieve this would be to redesign the seat. The initial seat used in the prototype had a very thick back and he felt sure that this could be reduced. However, when he approached the designers, they promptly told him to leave well alone, saying that it could not be done. The seats were comfortable and he could not have everything. This did not deter Alec: since they would not do the job, he would do it himself. When the two weeks were up, the cars were returned to the factory, each having completed some 10,000 miles. They had run well, and the drivers were extremely pleased with the results, having pushed them to the limit without any faults developing. All seemed to be well – until the de-briefing.

It then transpired that each driver had had to change the front brake pads during the two weeks, but it was not until they were all together that this was discovered. Each one of them had thought that he had just been a bit heavy footed with the new car. But it was more serious than that: on checking their cars again, they discovered that the front brake pads were down to the bare minimum, in particular the one located on the inside.

They all set about stripping their disc brake units, inspecting all the parts very carefully, but no faults could be found. The units were reassembled with harder brake pads and put back on the cars, and they went out for another week's testing. Unfortunately the fault was still there.

Time was running out fast and they had come up against a problem for which nobody had a cure, a problem which they could not brush to one side as if it had never happened. They had to find out what was behind it. Again the units were stripped but this time all the specifications and measurements of all the parts were examined carefully and checked against the blue prints. They felt sure that the fault was in the caliper. Disc brakes were new to the production car and they had never really been tested by the Rootes Group until now. They were all beginning to think they should not have bothered with them.

It was known that Healeys had started to use disc brakes and so discrete enquiries were made to see if they had come up against this obstacle. As it turned out, they had, and since they too had found no explanation as to why it was happening, they were only too willing to combine forces to find a cure. Alec contacted all the major brake component manufacturers, Lockheed, Dunlop, and Girling, and asked them to send their technical experts to a meeting he was arranging. This unorthodox approach did not exactly meet with their approval, but they knew they had to attend in an attempt to gain the contract to supply the parts. It was already agreed that the Healey representative would be allowed to attend.

The most amazing fact to come out of the meeting was that each company knew about the unusually fast rate of wear in the disc pads but each had kept this fact to itself. Every company had spent a great deal of time and money investigating the problem without success and seemed to push it to one side. It took the power of the Rootes Group, led by Alec, to bring this out into the open.

Lengthy discussions took place, each representative giving the others a run down of what tests they had carried out and what they had found. But at the end of the day they were no further forward. It was agreed that another meeting would be arranged, this time to try out each of the company's products under test conditions, and Alec started looking for a suitable location.

Anstie Airfield was hired for the testing, which was to carry on until the fault and its cure were found. A large number of people were now involved and other Rootes project engineers took the opportunity to try out their own models, which had been fitted with disc brakes. The vehicles were driven round the old airfield continuously, day and night, everyone involved taking his turn at the wheel. The brakes were checked every couple of days, each vehicle being allocated a log book to keep a record of its drivers to eliminate any possibility of heavy footedness. After several weeks of hard testing they realized that something was wrong: the pads were not wearing as quickly as they had previously. It gave the brains of the team something to grapple with and a conference was called. All the log books were checked and compared with the logs which had been kept by the drivers of the initial road test cars. After examining every possible aspect, the conference concluded that the only difference between the two tests was the fact that it had rained on the initial test but had been sunny and dry throughout the new tests. It was not a lot for them to work on, but there again they had nothing else.

Alec contacted the local council and hired a road sprayer which they used to keep the track wet. Once again, the cars drove round and round the airfield on their 24-hour vigil. It became somewhat monotonous for the drivers but they knew there was no other way. And to everyone's relief, after four days of hard driving, they had found the cause of the problem. It was obvious that they were not going to find the cure overnight, and as the bill for hiring the road sprayer was mounting up, Jeff Johnson, one of the team, suggested that they buy one. The one he had in mind was admittedly not the most modern, but at least it was cheap – £250. Alec had been recalled to the factory to give a situation report and he took the opportunity to ask Peter Ware (director of

Geoff Johnson with his road sprayer, bought by Rootes as part of their long and costly test programme to cure excessive wear on the disc brakes. (Alec Caine).

engineering) if he could buy the road sprayer. His first reaction was, 'You must be mad', but when Alec told him how much the hire costs were, he soon changed his mind. Jeff contacted the owners of what turned out to be a basic water carrier, and arranged to have it collected and taken to the works to have it converted into a sprayer. This gave Alec a chance to have a look at those seats again, to see if he could gain some extra leg room. It gave the rest of the team a chance to take a break from driving.

With only a few months in hand before the press release, arrangements had to be made to start production, using the existing brake components. Any changes that might be required would have to be incorporated later on. This state of affairs was not what anyone wanted, but there was no alternative.

Now they knew that water was the cause of the brake wear, the experts were able to do their home work. It transpired that the fault lay in the design of the backing plate which was supposed to have stopped all the road grime and water from getting to the discs and pads. An air hole which was in the centre of the backing plate was allowing a minimum amount of water and grime in, and once inside it had no escape. As the road wheels turned, the damp grime stuck to the disc.

This, coupled with the four thou. running clearance of the brake pads, turned the disc into a grinding wheel, and a very efficient grinding wheel at that.

Returning to Anstie together with the water carrier, all the team had to do now was to find the cure. Unfortunately, it was not as simple as just blocking up the hole! Using extra strong card, sellotape and staples to make up and test thousands of different backing plate designs, it was to take them over 18 months to come up with the final solution. Undoubtedly, this was the most expensive project Rootes and the brake manufacturers had ever tackled, but if it had not been for those men, disc brakes might not be used today. It did not take long for the word to spread round the motor manufacturers, many of whom telephoned Alec

Lockheed must have been disappointed when the contract for the Alpine's braking system went to Girling. They acquired one of the original test cars and used it to continue their own development programme, hoping to persuade Rootes to change their minds. But the Girling system remained with the Alpine throughout production. (Alec Caine)

for the cure (and that included Rolls-Royce). Girling got the contract to supply the brakes, but Lockheed did not give up that easily. Although the brakes were now wearing at an acceptable rate, they considered that there was still room for improvement and continued the testing (not at Anstie but by general touring) up until 1962, using one of the pre-production Alpines as their test vehicle.

The scheduled release of the Alpine had been arranged for 2nd July, the day after the conclusion of the Alpine Rally, and was to take place in Cannes. As the day drew nearer, everyone concerned could take things a bit easier while the first batch of pre-production models was assembled. Alec had time to make a few alterations to the seats and gained that extra inch he was looking for by narrowing the seat back. These alterations were incorporated in the new cars, which were now registered XVC 1 to XVC 12 consecutively and made ready for running in at the testing ground. Rootes' management had given Armstrongs the go-ahead to start building up a workforce of about 700 to man the production lines. Some of the jobs went to aircraft workers made redundant by Armstrongs' sister firm, Armstrong Whitworth, and they also advertised nationally for skilled body-finishers, trimmers, welders, electricians and assemblers. There was no shortage of applicants; they came from all over the country.

One question raised by the team was how they were going to get 12 brightly coloured, spotlessly clean cars with consecutive registration numbers to Cannes without being noticed. As they found out, not easily.

For some unknown reason they decided to drive in convoy to Lydd Airport in Kent where a transporter plane would fly them to France. Admittedly they got as far as Reigate without incident, then, blue flashing lights appeared in the driving mirrors and all at once the entire group was the centre of attraction. Being stopped by the police was one hazard they had not taken into account. Apparently several reports had been made about all these unusual cars travelling together, all bearing the same registration numbers. It took some explaining, and the entire group was held by the roadside until their story was checked out – still trying not to be noticed.

They eventually arrived in France, only to be ordered to return to Britain. Clearance to bring the cars into France had not been sought and the airport officials would not allow the group to continue, thinking that they were part of a commercial venture. It rapidly became obvious that no matter how hard they tried, they just could not convince the officials that the vehicles were not going to be sold. They were allowed one phone call, and decided to call the British Consul who instructed them to stay where they were while he sorted it out. Time was of the essence: the

Eleven pre-production Alpines, with the registration numbers XVC 1 to 11, were flown to the north of France, from whence they were driven to Cannes for the announcement.

announcement was less than three days away and with almost a day's driving yet to do, their timetable could well have been thrown out of the window. They waited patiently, the hours ticked by, and then they were told suddenly that they could leave. Alec recalled those long hours: 'We thought we would never be allowed entry. We were told it took some persuasive talking by the Ministry in London with the French Government. We were glad to get out of there and continue on our way, time was so short.'

They had a lot of time to catch up as they had arranged to stay overnight in an hotel halfway to Cannes. They eventually arrived just after midnight, hungry and tired, to be met by a very sympathetic hotel staff who served them dinner at 1 a.m. They then had a short sleep before continuing their journey. Shortly after leaving the hotel Alec spun his Alpine on gravel and damaged a front wing. It began to look as though somebody somewhere did not want them to make this journey.

After hammering the panel straight with two large stones, he managed the final leg to Cannes without incident. Norman Garrard had arranged parking under cover at a local dealer. Space was very limited, and nobody wanted to risk driving into the bays, since, as Alec remarked, 'with our luck something was bound to have happened'. Instead, the cars were pushed in, 'packed like sardines and the doors promptly locked'. For the first time since the journey started, they could all now breath a sigh of relief.

Everyone was up early the next morning, cleaning and preparing the ten cars to be used for the announcement which was only a few hours away. It was attended by representatives from most motoring magazines throughout the world and was followed by a mountainous drive from Cannes to St. Maxime, selected by Norman Garrard to enable the journalists to put the Alpine through its paces. The day finished with a dinner party, after which many of the journalists headed north for the

The announcement was timed to ensure maximum coverage from motoring journalists, who were already in the south of France to report on the French Grand Prix. Below: Lord Rootes with one of the ten cars on display, and overleaf: *giving the announcement.*

French Grand Prix. Some were luckier than others, having talked their way into being allowed to keep and use the Alpines for the remainder of their stay in France, promising to return them to the factory in one piece after they had tested them to the full.

The announcement had been a great success, after such an inauspicious start, and the team stayed on in Cannes for a few days holiday before returning to England by train – all except Timothy Rootes that is (the son of Sir Reginald and in charge of the servicing department). He had decided to take a full touring vacation in the South of France, using XVC 1. Unfortunately, no sooner had the team arrived back at the factory when they received a telephone call saying that he had broken the propshaft on his car and wanted it repaired immediately. They took the one off the prototype and found a couple of volunteers (which was no problem) to fly out and fit it.

The Alpine got better than average reviews from the press, and from the mass of orders Rootes received it soon became obvious that the

Inside the production lines of Bristol Siddeley Engines Ltd. After the initial piecing together of the bodywork, the cars were cleaned by hand and sent through to the painting tunnel. (Rolls-Royce Ltd.)

After leaving the painting tunnels, they went through the inspection stage, where any vehicles with paint flaws were taken off the lines. (Rolls-Royce Ltd.)

They then went through to the trimming department . . . (Rolls-Royce Ltd.)

where each man was responsible for one particular item. (Rolls-Royce Ltd.)

Once trimmed, the car's body was lifted and lowered onto the engine and back axle unit. (Rolls-Royce Ltd.)

After the engineering components had been bolted on, the car was ready to be driven away to the final inspection bays. Very few changes have been made to the way production lines are organized, and this method is still being used. (Rolls-Royce Ltd.)

demand was there. In fact, it proved necessary to build up the workforce of the Armstrong factory and start a night shift. There was no shortage of applicants, a good number of them coming from B.M.C. at Birmingham. By the end of August 1959, Rootes officials announced that future production was assured for many months on the basis of present orders alone, while the rate of orders from the U.S.A. and other dollar areas had already reached a level of 32 million dollars a year.

Alec Caine was never happy about the amount of leg room available for the driver. A tall man himself, he was always looking for ways to improve it, and was encouraged in this by several of the journalists at the announcement. In fact, it was to become something of an obsession with him: he wanted to be able to offer the Alpine to a larger proportion of the general public by catering for the taller than average person, something which other car manufacturers did not do.

Alec had been pestering the design department to find a suitable modification to gain a little extra legroom. As they appeared to show no interest, he continued to look for the solution himself. He was due to attend the Turin Motor Show as a representative of the Rootes Group and decided to combine the trip with a visit to a close friend at Superleggera Touring Milano, to see if they could help with the problem. Better known for building bodies for Ferrari, Aston and Jensen, Superleggera had gained an enviable reputation in the fields of design and development, and Alec knew that if they could not come up with any ideas he might as well give up.

He drove down to Turin in time for the opening of the show on 31st October 1959, using one of the pre-production models in order to give Superleggera something to work on. It also gave him the chance to test out a special camshaft which Rootes' competition department had designed to give the car more power. After the drive Alec rejected the idea of putting it into production cars.

Superleggera took a great interest in the Alpine and Alec's project. After discussing the modifications Alec had previously carried out, prior to production, it seemed as though there was nothing that could be done without making extensive alterations to the interior. They then suggested lowering the pedals. Although they knew that this would not gain much, Alec was willing to accept any additional room he could get. Alec left it in their hands and told them to try it. They managed to gain around 1½in., a bit more than Alec had anticipated, as he had thought that the modification would interfere with the operation of the clutch.

On returning to the works at Coventry, he showed the Superleggera design to the production designers. Standing there, looking at the finished product, they still insisted it could not be done. Although Alec was furious at the time, he won in the end, as the modification was used later on the Series 2 Alpine.

Rootes took note of any criticisms in road test reports as a guideline for further improvements. Nothing was missed out – even a passing comment from one of the journalists would be examined in detail to see what improvements could be made. Obviously they did not confine their attention to the journalists' comments alone, but handing a car over for a thorough road test was certainly one of the best, quickest (and cheapest) methods of sounding out public opinion. Motoring journalists are, after all, paid to criticize and find faults, and to give an unbiased point of view of the facts as they see them. Fortunately the Alpine never received a bad road test and those faults that were pointed out, were rectified. Hence, very few changes were made to the Alpine throughout its entire production life.

Although Alec and his team were always looking for ways to improve the Alpine, they were not too concerned with uprating its power output. They knew that this could be achieved quite easily, but the Rootes management were not interested in performance for performance's sake. First and foremost, they wanted to supply a low cost car which provided luxuries and comforts never seen before in a sports car of its class. Few would deny that they achieved this aim, and even by today's standards the Alpine's fitments and layout take some beating.

The Alpine's interior layout could certainly compete with that of even the most expensive cars.

On both the Series 1 and 2, the detachable hard top was an optional extra.

The Series 2 Alpine was introduced at the 1960 Motor Show, with very few changes. Alec's plan to lower the pedals had not been rejected by the designers as he had first thought. Instead, they had had a few ideas of their own and completely redesigned the seat. Together, the two modifications gained an extra $3\frac{1}{2}$ inches. The original design of the pillarless door windows came in for a rethink after long term tests revealed vibration when the sealing strip along the leading edge of the windscreen became worn. The metal channel which was added to the door also gave added support to the rather heavy window. The only other noticeable alteration was to the way the lid on the centre armrest opened – nobody can now remember why this change was considered necessary!

A great deal of minor changes were made to the mechanics, only two of which are of any significance to owners. Firstly, engine capacity was increased by 98 c.c. to 1592 c.c., for which Rootes claimed an increase in maximum torque by 5 per cent and maximum power by $2\frac{1}{2}$ per cent.

No-one would dispute the increase in torque, but the increase in power was negligible. Indeed, it would only be noticeable if a Series 1 and Series 2 Alpine were tested side by side under identical weather/road conditions. The other major change was to the rear suspension. In an attempt to obtain an acceptable compromise between comfort and road holding, the rear springs of the Series 2 were increased in width but decreased in depth, giving a firmer ride.

The relationship between the project engineers and the production designers at Rootes was non-existent, or so it seemed. Most modification projects put forward by Alec normally obtained a negative response. He accepted this, however, in the sure knowledge that whatever he said would not be forgotten.

One project for which neither team could claim responsibility started shortly after the introduction of the Series 2. Rumours had reached the Rootes factory that Superleggera had not only converted the pedals for

With the introduction of the Series 2 came the larger, 1600-c.c. engine. The only external alterations that can be seen are the channels along the leading edge of the door windows.

THE AUTOCAR, 20 JANUARY 1961

'IT'S A BEAUT' SAYS JACK BRABHAM

WORLD CHAMPION RACING DRIVER 1959 AND 1960

SUNBEAM ALPINE

now with 1·6 litre engine

POWER AND GRIP – that's the first impression I had when I tried this great Sunbeam Alpine. Whatever the road was like, you certainly felt that the lively Alpine had things well in hand. This sports car makes you feel good – the road streams away behind you and you know she's got all four corners well down.'

MORE POWER Lively 1592 cc engine develops 85·5 b.h.p., more torque – giving vivid acceleration and ample power.

MORE STABILITY Rear springs are bigger – for greater lateral stability. Larger capacity rear shock absorbers improve ride control and prevent fade.

MORE ROOM There is an extra 1½" between seat and steering wheel, the pedals are adjustable and the seats move farther back.

MORE REFINEMENTS Better weather sealing . . . detachable hood cant rails . . . an extra interior light . . . eight *less* greasing points . . . quick-action petrol filler cap.

Wire Wheels, White Wall Tyres, Overdrive and Hard-Top are optional extras. You can now choose from *five* colour schemes.

PRICE £695 plus P.T. £290.14.2

By Appointment
to Her Majesty The Queen
Motor Vehicle Manufacturers
Rootes Motors Limited

ROOTES MOTORS LTD

Sunbeam-Talbot Ltd., Coventry.
London Showrooms & Export Div. Rootes Limited,
Devonshire House, Piccadilly, London W.1

Alec but had been intrigued by the possibilities of finding other conversions which they could market themselves. As the Alpine was a very successful car, they would have no problems finding buyers. In particular, it was rumoured that Superleggera had found a way of increasing the luggage capacity of the boot, and for once the designers wanted to know more. After talking to Alec, they agreed to have a car booked in at Superleggera for the conversion to be carried out.

Alec drove the car down to Milan, arriving on Sunday evening and ready to take it in to the works the first thing Monday morning. When he visited Superleggera that morning, they were already converting an Alpine for one of their local customers. Alec was fascinated by what they were doing – it seemed to be such a simple but effective idea. He was told that they would not be able to complete his car for two days, but when he duly returned on Wednesday he was rather annoyed to find that his car had not even been started. They were giving the locals priority

Alec Caine was always concerned by the Alpine's lack of boot space, and he was determined to find a way of increasing it.

In an attempt to sort out the problem, he took a Series 2 down to his friends at Superleggera Touring Milan: They suggested two modifications: uprighting the spare wheel . . . (Alec Caine)

and placing the fuel tanks in the rear wing recesses. They also chopped the rear wings, shortening the fins. (Alec Caine)

and had completed a further two cars since Alec's last visit. He was assured that his would be ready on Friday, and sure enough it was.

The spare wheel had been uprighted against what you would jokingly call the back of the rear seat. This, combined with the two petrol tanks which had been repositioned in the rear wing recesses, gave a luggage capacity that would have been the envy of many saloon car owners. Unbeknown to Alec, Superleggera had also carried out a conversion to the rear wings, chopping the rear fins so that they were almost vertical. Superleggera were renowned for their conversions, which mostly entailed a complete redesign of the body to the shape they felt it should be. Although they could not fault the Alpine's design in its entirety, they had their own ideas on improving its appearance. When Alec looked inside the car, he saw that their ideas had not stopped there: they had fitted a wooden dashboard and a wood-rimmed steering wheel. Scarcely believing it, he asked what else they had done, but he was assured that that was it.

On his return to England, the first people Alec showed the car to were the 'set 'em alight boys'. Bernard Unett recalled his immediate reaction: 'The changes they made were good, the ideas were good, but when we opened the boot, talk about laughing. The Italians were paying good money for what was no more than two metal waste paper bins attached by two pipes. They weren't even balanced; when you turned a corner, you lost petrol. But the idea was there and it gave the designers something to work on.'

The designers were also impressed. It didn't take them long to design proper petrol tanks which used up as much of the rear wing recess space as possible. This gave them the added bonus of larger fuel capacity, but they had problems getting them balanced. Their first attempt ended up with the boot being filled with 16 foot of tubing. This was eventually eliminated by designing a special petrol cap and repositioning the tubes which connected the tanks. The end result was a very neat and tidy boot with an impressive capacity.

The seats which had been specially designed for the Series 2 had come in for a great deal of criticism from the road testers. They complained that although they were perfectly comfortable on short journeys, the upright back made them completely unsuitable on long journeys. It appears that the designers shrugged this off as utter nonsense, claiming that it did not matter anyway as people did not use the cars for long distance driving. Numerous people tried to convince them otherwise but without success.

Peter Ware was discussing the Alpine with a Mr. Edwards who was then head man at British Aerospace, and he happened to mention these criticisms. Mr. Edwards was quick to point out that there was only one group of people who knew anything about designing seats suitable for long-distance travelling, and they were the aircraft seat manufacturers. He suggested Peter Ware should contact one of them, pointing out that as they were in a very limited market they would probably jump at the chance of trying something different.

The moment Peter Ware got back to the factory, he mentioned the idea to Alec and the development engineers. They all agreed it was a good idea. But they had their own designers to think about and wondered what their reaction would be. They'd had a completely negative reaction when they asked them to design another one themselves and the last thing they wanted to do was to upset them in any way. As it turned out, the designers were only too happy to have someone carry out the work for them. For such a small department, any assistance in easing the workload was appreciated.

Peter contacted Microcell Ltd., the manufacturers of the world famous Microcell aircraft seat, and put the idea forward. As Edwards had foreseen, they were only too willing to have a go, considering it a challenge. He arranged an appointment for Alec and the development engineers to meet Microcell's designers, Les Avis and Les Horrocks, to discuss the project.

The arrangement pleased Alec. After seeing some of Microcell's seat designs, he knew that they would get as near perfect a seat as possible, and he left them to get on with it. He had a few other projects he wanted to get on with, one of those being adjustable steering. Several different methods of adjustable steering were on the market at the time, and he wanted to see if he could find a way of having one of them incorporated into the Alpine's steering mechanism, to keep up with the demands of those drivers who liked to drive straight-armed.

Meanwhile, a minority group of Rootes Group workers had begun to strike at regular intervals, much to the annoyance of the majority. The workers concerned were from a Rootes subsidiary company, British Light Steel Pressings Ltd. of Warple Way, Acton, London. The Rootes family had begun to regret ever taking over the firm but at the time it had become necessary to increase their pressing division, to keep up with the demand for their vehicles. Until the beginning of 1961 Rootes had had very little industrial action. From the great number of people I have spoken to, it would appear that Rootes were considered excellent employers. True, they were always on the look-out for methods of cutting expenditure, but no one can blame them for that. The shop stewards at the Acton factory first learned how to shout strike back in 1959 when a couple of newly weds at the factory, who were night shift workers, asked to be transferred to day shift. This was done and

1,500 workers came out on strike! At a time when strikes were relatively rare, this one became known as the 'Honeymoon Strike'.

The project engineers and designers were probably the only people to benefit from the strikes, as they now had the opportunity to spend more time experimenting with various steering column mechanisms. They eventually decided that the sliding splined steering column was just what they were looking for. It gave them $2\frac{1}{2}$ inches of height adjustment which, when combined with the seat Microcell were still working on, would allow the owner to choose for himself the position most suitable for him. It did cause a few winces at management level when they discovered it was the most expensive to produce, but it went into production anyway.

The one thing the project team did not have to worry about was finding a method of increasing the Alpine's performance. The works competition department had already seen to that. They were already marketing two stages of engine tune for those looking for that little bit of extra power, and as Alec would not accept any increase in engine noise in the production model, he thought it best to leave it to the owner to decide. Any owner who wanted more speed, and was willing to put up with more noise, could have the conversion carried out after he bought the vehicle.

For the first time since the introduction of the Alpine, Rootes had decided that the next series would be split into two models, one a Sports Tourer fitted with the soft top, and the other a Gran Turismo fitted with

The Series 3 Alpine was produced in two versions — the Gran Turismo, as shown here, and the Sports Tourer. The G.T. had a detachable hard top but no soft top.

The Sports Tourer had no hard top. Its soft top could be stowed away using the same method as on the earlier cars.

a removable hard top but no soft top. This gave Alec and the designers a chance to add a few extra refinements to the Gran Turismo, such as the wooden dashboard, steering wheel and other items which were vulnerable to damp and thus not advisable in a soft top model.

The designers had been working on a new hard top design which incorporated rear quarterlights. This gave better visibility and kept the Alpine's design in line with current trends. It not only changed the overall shape of the car, but gave it the appearance of being more spacious inside, even though the extra space gained was negligible.

Strikes at the Acton factory continued, and on 1st September 1961, 1,000 workers walked out again, bringing the total stoppages since 1st January 1961 to 82. These were crippling the Rootes Group and there was nothing they could do about it. The strikes, which were mainly unofficial and against union advice, had caused the loss of over 27,000 man hours at the Acton factory, which in turn had caused the loss of 17,000 man hours at other factories. This latest strike was called because of 'fears of extensive short time working and large scale redundancy'. When management refused to hold talks with the men's leaders (not the unions), they walked out.

On Monday, 4th September 1961, the strikers decided to send delegates to the T.U.C. Annual Conference at Portsmouth, to try to persuade the T.U.C. to adopt a new national policy in relation to the car industry. They wanted 52 weeks pay per year for all workers in the car industry, no matter what the situation. They also told the T.U.C. that they did not want any interference by union officials. 'We feel this has been allowed to develop as a local problem because of lack of action from outside and we think we are in a better position to get a settlement with our management', a spokesman told *Acton Gazette* reporters. He continued, 'We don't want the type of assistance the union officials gave us last time, when we stopped work over a short time dispute. On the first day we stopped, we were ordered back to work without anybody considering why we had come out.' The strike delegates achieved nothing at the conference. By 18th September 1961, the strike had brought the Rootes Group almost to a standstill, with over 6,000 workers from the various Coventry factories being laid off.

Only the non-production line staff continued to work and that included Alec, his team and the designers. The way the strike was going, it would be a long time before the Series 3 Alpine could be introduced. This gave them even more time to examine and try out an almost incredible number of different components. The Microcell seats were now taking shape, and certainly nobody would be able to say they were not sufficiently adjustable. They could be moved forward and backward 7 inches and reclined into four positions, while the front could be raised or lowered $\frac{3}{4}$ inch and the rear 1 inch. The seat did away with the conventional coil springs altogether, incorporating sectional foam blocks. As it made the driver sit considerably lower in the car, Alec had the foresight to realize that the existing control pedals might cause some problems. He decided that this should be investigated at once, as they would not be able to introduce one without the other.

Until now, Lord Rootes had refused to comment on the strike, but on 26th September 1961, he made his first statement to the workers concerned: 'Return to work by Thursday or be sacked.' The strikers ignored the threat, and on Thursday, 28th September 1961, all 1,000 workers were sacked. A recruitment drive was started to replace the striking workers. The strikers objected to this, protesting that the Acton Labour Exchange was engaged in strike-breaking by sending men down to the factory for jobs – jobs which, as the committee said, 'They will go back to, once the management accepts to abide by the rules of the committee.' Rootes replied: 'We regard the strikers as ex-employees. We have invited applications for their jobs. Some strikers have re-applied and we believe others will follow.'

How to get a Sunbeam Alpine ready for winter:

(1) Roll up the windows.

Oh, yes...and put in some anti-freeze.

NOVEMBER, 1961

9

The Rootes Group had complete backing from all their other employees, from the unions, and from the wives of the strikers (this was given a great deal of publicity). But the sacked strikers would not listen, stating that 'We are determined to see it through.' As the weeks rolled on, 8,000 workers from other factories were made redundant. Rootes were now having financial problems, and it was in fact the beginning of the downfall of the Rootes empire. Controlled by five men, the strike had caused irreparable damage to the Rootes Group and its finances. There was a call for a public enquiry after it was disclosed that the strike was Communist planned and directed.

Brian Rootes announced that Superleggera were to start producing the Alpine for the Italian market. This would at least clear some of the back log of orders that was steadily building up. They would also be building a limited number of Hillman Minxes. By 2nd November 1961, Rootes had found other manufacturers to supply them with the body panels that should have been produced at the Acton works. They had also re-engaged 1,750 workers at their Coventry factories in an attempt to get the production lines rolling once more. The strikers from what was now labled 'the dead duck strike' were gradually drifting back, and by 30th November, Acton's work force was up to 680, 430 of whom had been strikers. By December 21st 1961, only 120 men were still out. After a final meeting, they decided to go back, but Rootes turned them away, giving them £40 compensation as a token gesture. Only one of the strike committee members was re-employed.

The dispute may have been over, but it was only the start of the Rootes Group's problems. Their first priority was to build up their workforce to enable them to fulfil the outstanding orders.

The Alpine's engineers had been searching through the parts division to find suitable control pedals. They were looking for something with a large foot pad which could fit straight into the Alpine without major modification. It was a long shot, but with finances being what they were, everyone was economizing. After trying various types which could not be set up at the right angle to suit the new seat, they tried those from the Sapphire. They appeared to be a perfect fit, at least for the longer legged members of the team. The remainder were not happy with them, however, thinking that they were just too low for comfort. A compromise was reached by having an extra 'knuckle' added to the rear of the pedal shafts. This allowed the pedal to be raised and lowered, giving a variation of $1\frac{7}{8}$ inches: it may not sound much on paper, but in reality it makes a considerable difference.

In an attempt to cut expenditure, the management had decided to move production of the Alpine to the Ryton-on-Dunsmore plant just

Superleggera's modifications of the boot layout were incorporated in the Series 3, giving it a luggage capacity equivalent to that of a saloon car. For some reason, Rootes did not take up their suggestion to chop the rear wings until the introduction of the Series 4.

outside Coventry. It had also become necessary to delay the introduction of the Series 3, as they already had sufficient orders outstanding to keep production of the Series 2 going for over 12 months.

A great many minor mechanical changes were to be introduced with the Series 3. These included the replacement of the level-arm type shock absorbers on the rear suspension by telescopic dampers, coupled with a slight alteration to the spring dimensions. This made the vehicle 'nicely taut and perfectly balanced, asking to be tossed about', according to *Car and Driver* (October 1963). It had been decided that the exhaust manifold of the G.T. would be made of cast iron rather than tubular steel as on the Sports Tourer, to reduce noise. Some export models were also to be fitted with large aircleaners. In all, these changes lost the G.T. some 7 b.h.p. – power which was not to be replaced – all for the sake of quietness.

They had finally conquered the problems of the front disc brakes, primarily by designing and proving a new splashguard. They also

THE SUNBEAM IS A RAINDROP

When you're looking for perfection, you look to nature. Aerodynamically, the raindrop, at its moments of swiftest descent, is nature's most perfect shape—for it is then that it most closely resembles the theoretically ideal teardrop. And it was only a matter of time before the record breakers at Bonneville, as well as at the other important race circuits, would learn the lessons that nature has to teach. ¶ It's an easy lesson to learn, too, if you think of air in terms of *substance*—as if there were a constant sandstorm or hailstorm. For air is a conglomeration of material things that offer resistance to whatever moves through it. And that is one of the reasons why aerodynamics is so important in the design of planes and rockets. And one of the reasons why aerodynamics or correct streamlining is so important to the design of high-speed automobiles. ¶ It is also one of the reasons why the Sunbeam Alpine is designed the way it is. ¶ Obviously no car—except for express-purpose record assaulters—can be designed exactly like a drop, incorporating all the aerodynamic considerations that will permit it to approach perfection. It must have headlights, headroom, breadth for at least two people, an exposed underside for easy accessibility, attractive trim, practical door handles, exposed tire area, and a rear end that includes luggage space. All these, plus the windshield configuration, hubcaps, fenders, bumpers, grille, mirrors, even the kind of body paint, which produces skin friction, interact with each other and contribute the total air resistance of a car. ¶ But all of these components can be designed to approximate, as closely as possible, nature's dictum as expressed in her design of the drop. ¶ Notice how, in the Sunbeam Alpine configuration, designers have not wandered far from nature's laws of aerodynamics. Only to make the car practical have compromises been admitted — and these sparingly and brilliantly. ¶ See how the trailing edge of the drop has been faired in and blunted by nature? See the Sunbeam Alpine. See how the leading edge of the drop has been smoothly rounded by nature? See the Sunbeam Alpine. See how, in the drop, there is a smooth, continuous, uninterrupted flow of air surface from one end to the other? See how this is accomplished in the Sunbeam — more so with the amendment of rear quarter fins that add not only to the car's aerodynamic efficiency, but to the sweeping grace of its lines, as well. ¶ The useful and the beautiful have been masterfully blended in the Sunbeam Alpine to achieve the practical ultimate in sports car design. It is for this reason that Sunbeam Alpine has won the Index of Thermal Efficiency at Le Mans, that it took first in its price class at Sebring, that it swept its class at Riverside, at Danville, at Bridgehampton, at Laguna Seca—at major events in the U.S. and all over the world. ¶ And, since imitation is the sincerest form of flattery, we are not displeased at seeing other marques beginning to copy this law of nature and innovation of Sunbeam design—the kind of advanced structuring that makes Sunbeam Alpine one of the world's outstanding cars. For the incomparable excitement of driving a truly fine sports car, test the Alpine at your Sunbeam Alpine dealer's. It can be yours for only $2595.*

SUNBEAM ALPINE A DESIGN OF DISTINCTION BY ROOTES

*East poe, slightly more in West.   State, local taxes, delivery charge, if any, white walls optional, extra.

61

increased the diameter of the disc by 0.35 inches and gave the brakes servo assistance. It had certainly turned out to be the longest experimental test ever carried out on one single item, with so many manufacturers involved. They all wanted to ensure that the disc brake system was perfected, to make it both an efficient and an economical proposition.

In November 1962, Rootes announced the total cost of the Acton strike up until the year ending 31st July. They showed a loss of £891,088, compared with a profit of nearly £3 million the previous year. This type of loss Rootes could not afford. They were already heavily committed to a new project, the Hillman Imp, and the opening of a new plant at Linwood in Scotland where it was to be produced. This turned out to be the biggest phase of expansion in the group's history, and losses at this time were the last thing Rootes wanted.

Production of the Series 3 Alpine started in January 1963, although it was not introduced to the public until March 1963. One of the modifications Superleggera had carried out on Alec's car, the chopped

Halfway through the Series 3, the Alpine's Zenith carburettors were replaced by the twin-choke Solex, which continued to be used throughout the Series 4. It was not everyone's choice of carburation. (Mike Green)

rear fins, was not included in the new model. For reasons best known to themselves, the management decided to hold onto this for future models. The Series 3 was initially fitted with the twin Zenith carburettors, but from July these were replaced by a single twin choke Solex compound carburettor (from chassis no. B9204718). This, they claimed, would increase economy and give extra power when needed. This may have been true when the carburettors were new (although road tests show it was not), but after a short time the carburettors became worn and were very difficult to keep in tune. The choice could not have been worse. Far better carburettors were on the market at the time, but company policy dictated that they were not to be made available for use on the Alpine.

The Series 3 became the shortest lived of all the Alpines, with production lasting less than a year. The designers at Rootes and at Superleggera had joined forces to come up with a number of minor styling changes to introduce what was then to be the Series 4 Alpine. The chopped rear fin was to be introduced with a new front grille consisting of one horizontal bar with a small centre badge. The over-riders

The redesigned rear fin, as suggested by Superleggera, was eventually used on the Series 4, updating the Alpine's appearance. (Mike Green)

were updated and made smaller with rubber inserts. The only other noticeable changes were the introduction of a Monza style petrol cap, and a new front sidelight unit, as current lighting regulations dictated that sidelight and indicator lights should work independently of each other.

The new car was first introduced by Superleggera at the Turin Motor Show in November 1963. This was quickly followed by Rootes' announcement at the Brussels Motor Show in January 1964. The most controversial point was the introduction of an automatic gearbox into a sports car. Built with the American market in mind, the Series 4 was the first sports car of its kind to be imported into the United States. It certainly raised eyebrows over here, where Douglas Armstrong writing for *Modern Motoring And Travel* (June 1964) summed up the initial reaction: 'Oh yes, the aficionados will tell you an automatic transmission is just not on for a sports car – that it will pull down the performance, drink petrol, and not provide the control necessary for exploiting the car to the full. I'll confess I used to feel this way and speaking as an enthusiast I know that it is all bound up with the racing driver "image",

The G.T. models were fitted with wooden dashboards and carpeting, whereas the S.T. models retained the plastic dashboard and rubber matting because of the possibility of rain penetration through the soft top. (Mike Green)

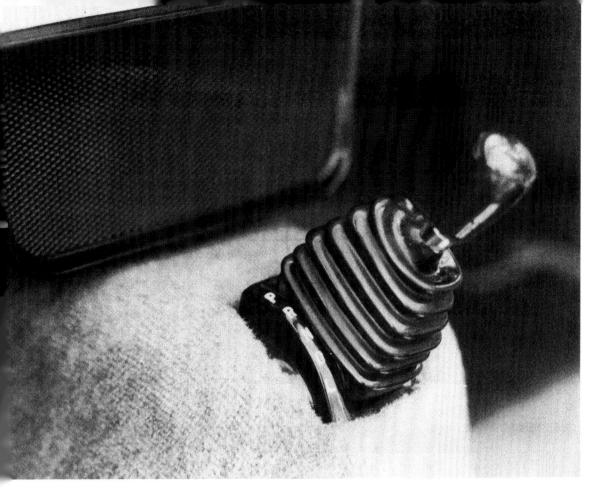

For the first time in a sports car, Rootes introduced an automatic gearbox in the Series 4 Alpine. The novel idea of the gear change stick was well accepted. (Mike Green)

that all keen sports car drivers carry in their heads – whether they'll admit it or not! Unless they can go into that fastish bend in third gear over-run with the engine roaring and a general Grand Prix-type aura all around, then the whole thing is too dull for words. I know the feeling, and love it, but Borg-Warner's type 35 transmission cannot be as lightly dismissed as all that.'

He then went on to talk about acceleration figures: 'It is a fact that all automatics absorb a little of the engine power, but such is the speed of the gear change that there is little difference in the acceleration figures of the manual and Borg Warner models. I found I could easily get 0 – 60 m.p.h. in 15 seconds and 0 – 50 m.p.h. in 10.5 secs.' These figures quoted by Mr. Armstrong differ considerably from those given by other motoring journals such as the tests in *Motor* (10.10.64). They had times of 0 – 50 m.p.h. in 13 seconds and 0 – 60 m.p.h. in 18 seconds, whereas

Autocar (22.5.64) achieved 0 – 50 m.p.h. in 13.3. seconds and 0 – 60 m.p.h. in 18.8 seconds. Bearing in mind that these tests were carried out on the same car, the differences are considerable, although not as great as the differences in top speeds. While *Motor* got 98.8 m.p.h., *Autocar* only managed 92 m.p.h.

In his article, Douglas Armstrong explained how he got his figures: 'There is a trick for getting the best acceleration out of the type 35 transmissions – a sort of "viscount" technique. One keeps the left foot on the brake pedal, and with the car in gear, lift the revs with the accelerator. The fluid coupling won't allow the engine to rise more than about 1,200 r.p.m. while the brakes are on, but the moment the left foot is removed and the throttle is slammed down, off you go like a turbine – without time lag!' One begins to wonder if this was the reason for such differences in the figures! We will never know. The Series 4 was certainly slower compared to the Series 1 and 2 but slightly

The Microcell seats adjusted in every possible way, giving the driver a wide choice of driving positions and increasing leg room considerably. (Mike Green)

quicker than the heavy Series 3. But whichever way you look at it, is a difference of just over 1 m.p.h really that significant?

Alec's obsession for making a quieter, more luxurious car gradually reduced the engine power. All the modifications he had carried out were effective, even though the car was never noisy in the first place, but nothing was done to compensate for the loss of power. This came in for some criticism, not so much from the press, but from the team itself. They asked the engine development department to do something about it and were duly promised some improvement.

The Series 4 Alpine can be split into two models, the early Series 4 and the late Series 4. Come September 1964, some rather significant changes were made, one of which was the introduction of synchromesh on all forward gears (this had been introduced by other manufacturers some time previously). In addition, the trailing edges of the doors and bonnet were 'squared' off, which meant that it was no longer necessary to lead in the joints where the front wings met the scuttle panel, and where the outer sill met the front and rear wings. This was supposed to have been done to speed up production, but one suspects that the real reason was to cut down costs.

Apart from the shortened rear wings, the Series 4 was distinguished externally by the single horizontal bar, replacing the grille, and the new type of sidelights, introduced to keep up with regulations. (Mike Green)

On 30th September 1964, Lord Rootes announced that during October three representatives of the Chrysler Corporation would be joining the board of Rootes Motors Ltd. – Irving Minett, Group Vice-president, International Operations of the Chrysler Corporation; Lovis B. Warren, a director of Chrysler; and Robert C. Mitchell, President and Managing Director of Chrysler International. The move followed the acceptance by the shareholders of Rootes Motors Ltd. of the Chrysler Corporation's offer to acquire 30 per cent of the ordinary voting shares in the company and 50 per cent of the non-voting 'A' shares.

The first official news of the link came on 4th June when an agreement was reached in New York by Lord Rootes and Sir Reginald Rootes with Lynn A. Townsend, President of Chrysler, and George Love, Chairman of the Chrysler Board, concerning the proposed acquisition of the shares. Treasury consent to the proposals were given on 29th July by the Chancellor of the Exchequer, who at that time was Reginald Maudling.

In the formal letter to shareholders outlining the offer, issued on 10th August by S. G. Warburg Co. Ltd. on behalf of Chrysler, Lord Rootes stated that the Rootes board welcomed the Chrysler approach: in view of the intense and increasing competition in the motor industry at home and overseas, it was a logical and desirable step in the future development of the Rootes Group to become associated with a strong international organization such as Chrysler. On 29th September, Warburgs announced that they had received the necessary acceptances from the shareholders, and this was followed by Lord Rootes' statement regarding Chrysler representation on the board of Rootes Motors Ltd.

Although it has never been confirmed officially, it has always been suspected that this had all come about because of the Acton strike and Rootes' inability to recoup the losses involved. These may not have sounded that onerous at the time, but it must be remembered that the cost of building vehicles was not much less than the price they were being sold for (to make them competitive) and that breaking even on any project was a long, slow process.

Lord Rootes kept his workers informed as to what was actually taking place between Rootes and Chrysler, and when negotiations were finalized the following message was passed to all his employees, expressing his views on the situation: 'You will all have read by now of our partnership negotiations with the Chrysler Corporation which have resulted in this American motor manufacturer, the third largest in the United States and indeed in the world, acquiring an interest in Rootes Motors Ltd.

'I would therefore like to take this opportunity to declare that I and all the other members of the Rootes Board are confident that this association with Chrysler will prove to be the prelude to a period of great progress for the Rootes Group.

'It does not mean that the Rootes family interests, financial or otherwise, in Rootes Motors will be diminished in any way but rather that a real partnership is being established with Chrysler with a view to bringing advantages to all parties concerned.

'Among these advantages will be an increase in the scope and activities of the Rootes Group as far as both cars and commercial vehicles are concerned – and this in turn will offer wider opportunities to all our employees.

'You will all be asking exactly how we shall gain from this partnership with an American company. First of all we shall obviously benefit from our contact with the Chrysler Organization in America with its immense facilities and "know how" as far as engineering, research, production and other aspects of our industry are concerned.

'In this country, this will help to make us more competitive and more progressive and I anticipate that this will mean that the Rootes Group will be able to expand more rapidly.

'Abroad, the association is also going to stimulate our vitally important export sales as we shall be able to benefit from Chrysler's wide facilities in merchandizing and manufacturing throughout the world. There is no doubt that the present highly competitive climate in world markets calls for larger motor manufacturing groups.

'You will also be wondering exactly how this partnership will operate. We have, in fact, agreed with Chrysler that the existing management of the Rootes Group will continue while at the same time three Chrysler representatives will be appointed to our main board. In this way, we shall be able to co-ordinate policy and expansion both in the U.K. and world markets and work together to one another's advantage.

'As to the future, the Chrysler Corporation with their broad-minded approach to world trading, have already pledged, in a letter to the treasury, that they will not initiate any action to impair either the home or overseas operations or the management and direction under the Rootes Board of our company – or our relations with the government, labour, our British shareholders and the public.

'Finally I would like to say that as a frequent visitor to the United States over many years, I am very well acquainted with the Chrysler Organization and its products. I have long held them in high regard and I am confident that we are all going to make a good team, and that we shall create a happy and progressive partnership. I am also confident that everyone in our Group will contribute towards our efforts to take full advantage of the opportunities which this association is offering us – and that, perhaps not immediately but in time, it will bring great benefits to all of us.'

One can't help wondering just how much Lord Rootes really wanted this crucial development. It's hard to imagine that a man who had dedicated his life to building up an empire from nothing and against all odds, using methods that a great many people and manufacturers disapproved of at the time, but followed suit once they were proved successful, would want to give up such a large percentage of his business without feeling at least a little remorse.

Meanwhile, the engine development department had been fulfilling their promise to design a new and larger engine for the 'set 'em alight boys'. That they had not exactly been over-inventive was immediately apparent when they delivered about six units for testing and told them what they had done. Nobody was that enthusiastic when they heard that it was yet another overbore of the original unit, this time to 1725 c.c. They had hoped for something different. Surely, the engine which started off life back in 1954 as a 1390 c.c. unit could not possibly have that much left inside to take out? Not wishing to argue with the experts, they fitted one of the units to a car for testing. It was started, and they could hardly believe the din it made. It rattled and shook like an old tug boat. They were dismayed, to say the least, wondering just what they were expected to do with it. A second unit was stripped, examined, balanced, re-assembled, fitted and tried. The end result? The same as before. It was no good, even with their expertise they could not make something out of nothing, and they promptly sent the units back to the engine development department and asked them to try again.

Unlike car designs, new engine designs are very rarely introduced. Once a good basic design has been tried and tested, development goes on from there. However, there must be a time when major changes become essential, and for the Alpine's unit, that time had arrived. They had almost doubled the brake horsepower of the unit with very little effort, but there was no way they were going to succeed in getting more from it without updating the bottom end. Five-bearing crankshafts were now common on a lot of cars: they gave smoother running and had been well tested. Rootes had been slow to follow suit, but they had now no alternative. They did not really expect to get the results they obtained. With the five-bearing crankshaft, the engine was smooth, it retained its strength, and in all it brought a new lease of life to the over 20-year-old unit. The brake horsepower was boosted once again, but where did it all go to? If you read the results of the road tests, there was very little difference between the performance figures of the Series 5 compared to those of the smaller-engined Series 2, and in fact the top speed of the Series 2 was higher. I honestly cannot believe this to be true, as I have driven both and have always thought the Series 5 to be the faster car. But that is only a personal opinion. It is known that changing the shape of the hard top, and uprighting the windscreen to enable the change to be made, altered the car's aerodynamics, which naturally interfered with the drag co-efficiency, but would this have affected it this much? Nobody has been able to give me an answer, so it will have to remain a mystery.

On 12th December 1964, it was announced that Lord Rootes of Ramsey, Chairman of the Rootes Group, had died. Many tributes were paid to this great industrial leader from people in all walks of life, including representatives from all his major competitors. Sir Reginald Rootes was elected Chairman in succession, and Geoffrey Rootes, now the second Lord Rootes, elder son of the late Lord Rootes, became Deputy Chairman.

Many people have said that it was the late Lord Rootes who dictated company policy and, indeed, who held the Group together. However, it soon became obvious that not everyone was in agreement as to the way the company had been run, and on 19th January 1965 it was announced that massive organization changes were to be made. Although a great number of employees did not like what was happening to the company, the teamwork carried on and, with it, the development of the

Safety tests played a vital part in the design of Rootes Group vehicles. The Alpine shown here is undergoing a crash test at M.I.R.A.

Series 5 Alpine. After many thousands of miles of testing, the only changes that were made to the new engine were to replace the dynamo by an alternator, and the twin choke Solex carburettor by twin Strombergs, which provided the engine with better performance and economy. Very few other changes took place, and the car body/interior design/lay-out remained basically the same as in the Series 4, although footwell ventilators were installed.

The Series 5 Alpine was announced in September 1965. Sales of the Alpine had declined considerably in the last year, with only 4,470 cars being sold. It was decided that the automatic gearbox version should be dropped as the expected demand from the U.S.A. had not materialized. It was a brave gamble and a gamble worth taking. The project had not been a complete flop, for a considerable number were built and sold.

The photo graphically reveals the strength and safety of the Alpine: after a headlong collision, the doors could still be opened, the bonnet had not gone through the windscreen, and the engine had not been affected. (The car used was the prototype of the Series 5, showing the 1725-c.c. engine — the only significant change that was made.)

Although the days of the 'set 'em alight boys' team were numbered, they continued to carry out their testing programme, always on the look-out for any faults, although by now, with the Alpine over seven years' old, there was little chance of that. They had covered many hundreds of thousands of miles and had examined virtually every part of the car, modifying and updating any parts that they even suspected might cause problems for owners in the future.

Alec continued to think of ways of improving the car. One of his last ideas was never put into use. Although the hard top of the G.T. was removable, it is a very heavy and cumbersome object to lift, and is definitely not the job for one man. Alec knew this and for some time had been working on an idea for a half hard top, half soft top. Basically his plan was that the outer edges of the standard hard top would be attached to the car, while a soft top section extended from the front windscreen to the rear boot line, allowing this section to be unzipped and rolled back, giving what can only be described as a full length sunroof. Although it was never put into production on the Alpine, the design was sold and with further development became known as the Targa hard top, now used on many vehicles.

During the financial year of 1966/7, the Rootes Group had accumulated enormous losses totalling £10 million. It became obvious to

One of the projects Alec worked on was a part hard top, part soft top. This was never put into production for the Alpine, but the idea was sold and later became known as the 'Targa style hard top'. (Alec Caine)

It was an ingenious design, giving virtually the best of both worlds. Alec designed it with the G.T. in mind, as he realized that many owners would have problems when they tried to remove the very heavy hard top. (Alec Caine)

The centre soft top section could be rolled back and then tucked away out of sight. These photos were taken a good number of years after the top was made and it looks somewhat tatty in its present state. However, Alec assures me that, when new, it was very smart and completely water-tight. (Alec Caine)

all that Chrysler would soon take over control of the Group. This actually took place in January 1967, when they increased their holding of voting shares to 77.3 per cent. It was now only a matter of time before the Rootes Group as such disappeared completely. In March 1967, Sir Reginald Rootes stepped down from office and Geoffrey (the second Lord Rootes) took his place as Chairman. Chrysler's Gilbert Hunt was then appointed Managing Director and given the job of reclaiming what was left of the once thriving Rootes empire.

Production of the Alpine Series 5 stopped in January 1968 and the marque has never been replaced. I have always wondered to what extent Chrysler were embarrassed by the Tiger's Ford engine, and, indeed, whether the Alpine story would have had a different and happier ending, had the Tiger never been produced. But that is something we will never know.

3
The Hybrids

THE HARRINGTON ALPINES

Thomas Harrington, a wheelwright, founded Thomas Harrington Ltd. at Brighton in 1897. The company grew steadily, going public when it became necessary to gain extra capital for expansion. Even so, it remained very much a family run concern, management being passed on to Thomas's sons, Ernest and Thomas, who in turn passed it on to their sons, Clifford, Gordon, Peter and Geoffrey, who looked after the company until its take-over in 1963.

The company's main business between the wars was building coach bodies on to chassis built by such firms as Dennis, Bedford and Commer. It was at this time that they decided to embark on a new venture by building special car bodies for the Ballot, Rolls-Royce and Talbot chassis. Harrington's pioneered the Weyman type of body construction, even before it was so christened. Developed in 1922 by a Frenchman named Charles T. Weymann, this was a type of bodywork in which the framing was made up of narrow sections of timber, fastened together by light metal strips instead of the conventional wooden joints. This permitted the structure to flex instead of crack, which had always been a problem with previous methods. In place of metal panelling, the framework was covered by leathercloth stretched over padding. Weymann, being a very wise man, patented the idea before Harrington's had even thought of doing so, thus ensuring that companies who wished to construct such bodies paid him a license fee. Apart from the coach and car building side of the business, the company became U.K. concessionaires for various overseas marques including Oldsmobile and Austro-Daimler, and finally became a main dealer for the Rootes Group.

By the time the Second World War broke out, business was flourishing and Harrington's had moved into a large purpose-built factory on the old Shoreham Road, Hove. Like all large coachbuilding firms, they contributed to the war effort by directing their energies towards an armament programme. They built military vehicles and airframes as well as carrying out prototype work for the War Office.

When the war ended, the company resumed its previous coachbuilding and commercial vehicle body building programme. It was not until March 1961 that another Harrington bodied car appeared – the Sunbeam Harrington Alpine (later to be known as the Harrington 'A' type Alpine).

The Harrington 'A' type Alpine, a fixed-head version introduced by Thomas Harrington Ltd. and shown here at its launch at their premises in Hove.

There had always been a close link between Thomas Harrington Ltd. and the Rootes Group, especially since they became a Rootes main dealer. This, coupled with the Alpine's quickly won reputation as a sports tourer which was a cut above its competitors, prompted Harrington's to re-enter the specialist car body building market, using the Alpine as a base. Under the command of Clifford Harrington, Harrington's skilled workforce had already built up a reputation for high quality products, and this was to be reinforced at the launch of the Harrington Alpine.

Based on the Series 2 Alpine, the Harrington incorporated a bolt-on, glass fibre, fast-back hard top. It could by no means be called a simple conversion, as the hard top was not added until extensive modifications were carried out to the interior and chassis. The strengthening cross member of the original Alpine, situated behind the rear seat (where the boot hinges are bolted to), was cut away and re-positioned further to the rear of the vehicle. The hinges of the abbreviated boot lid were bolted to this, as was the rear extremity of the new roof. Fitting the new roof provided more luggage space, which was fully carpeted, and increased the headroom by 2 inches. The prototype underwent extensive testing at M.I.R.A. and proved to have greater torsional rigidity over the standard Alpine. To the testers' surprise, there was a complete absence of drumming and wind noise, even at high speeds.

The Harrington 'A' type provided increased interior room and was offered with various choices of interior trim.

It had rear opening quarter lights to provide ventilation without draughts, but boot space was reduced.

It was intended that the Harrington Alpine be marketed in standard trim form, with the optional extra of trimming to customers' requirements. But because of the sudden influx of orders received after the announcement, most of the cars were personalized and very few were actually made in standard form. Apart from the various types of trim available as optional extras, three stages of engine tune were offered, the result of work carried out in conjunction with George Hartwell Ltd. The third stage was fitted with twin 40 D.C.O.E. Weber carburettors, with a 10.2 to 1 compression ratio. This was capable of over 110 m.p.h., and gave 0–60 m.p.h. in 10.6 seconds, and yet still returned around 22 m.p.g. when driven hard under test conditions.

The most prolific of the Harrington Alpines must be the Le Mans, which dropped the Alpine name from its title, and was known in the U.K. as the Sunbeam Harrington Le Mans, and in North America as the Sunbeam Le Mans G.T.

It was introduced at the Earls Court Motor Show in 1961 as a limited production model, in celebration of Harper and Proctor winning the Index of Thermal Efficiency at the 1961 Le Mans. The body conversion was more radical than the previous Harrington Alpine, being fitted with a glass fibre fixed head coupé style roof, which was bonded onto

Probably the most famous of the Harrington Alpines was the car entered in the 1961 Le Mans, shown here with Peter Harper, one of the drivers. It won the Index of Thermal Efficiency.

Following the success at Le Mans, Harringtons introduced the Sunbeam Harrington Le Mans. Although the car was based on the Sunbeam Alpine, the word 'Alpine' was never used in its title.

The Harrington Le Mans did away with the rear fins completely, and was fitted with a fibreglass roof which was bonded to the metal body — a process that many manufacturers had been trying to achieve for years without success.

cut-down rear wings, disposing of the fins completely, and incorporated a large rear window/cum luggage door which opened in the same way as modern hatchbacks do today. Being more security conscious, however, it could be opened only from the inside of the car, by means of a handle recessed into the trim panel just behind the driver's seat. Again, as with its predecessor, a large number of optional extras were available. There were five stages of engine tune – to the standard Le Mans specification, plus the three offered on the Harrington Alpine, and an extensive choice of interior trim. Possibly the most luxurious Le Mans was the one built for Prince William of Gloucester, who later tragically lost his life in an air crash. This was fitted with an all leather interior and a highly tuned engine, and was distinguishable externally by the egg box radiator grille. Only two Le Mans cars had that particular grille, the other being the company's own demonstration model.

Only two minor changes took place while the car was in production. The Harrington badges on the lower parts of the front wings were deleted from later models, as were the air extractors fitted aft of the rear quarterlight.

The first of the hatchbacks?

The amount of interior space was almost incredible. When the rear seats were folded forward, the car provided the luggage capacity of an estate car.

The engine of the Le Mans was allegedly tuned to the same specification as that of the car which ran in the 24-hour race.

Every Harrington was personalized according to the taste of the buyer.

The door panels incorporated an arm and knee rest and a side pocket.

The 'C' type Harrington Alpine was introduced as a follow on to the Le Mans, incorporating the opening tailgate type of top of the Le Mans, but retaining the rear fins of the original Alpine. An additional modification was introduced in the hard top – a rearward opening air vent, above the rear window/door, to improve ventilation. The roof, as with its predecessors, afforded all-round visibility and incorporated rearward opening quarterlights. Although several Harrington Le Mans cars were produced after the introduction of the 'C' type, they were gradually phased out. As the 'C' type was based on the Series 2 Alpine and introduced at the 1962 motor show, it had a short life. Production had to be stopped in February 1963, when the Series 2 Alpine was replaced by the Series 3. It is estimated that no more than a dozen of these cars were produced.

The introduction of the Series 3 Alpine, with its new style hard top which altered the slant of the windscreen frame, meant that a new mould was needed for the Harrington hard top. Apart from the cost, this took

After a limited production run, the Harrington Le Mans was replaced by the Harrington 'C' type Alpine. This bore the same style of hard top as the Le Mans but retained the Alpine's rear fins.

The only modification to the hard top was a roof vent, which increased ventilation and stability.

The concept of an egg crate grille originally came from Howes' prototype but was not used on the Alpine because of over-heating problems. Harringtons had overcome these.

All-leather interiors were not uncommon in the Harringtons, but can certainly cause problems if they have to be restored today.

some time to build. The 'D' type Harrington was first announced in June 1963. Advertising was very limited and like its predecessors, the 'A' and 'C' types (but unlike the Le Mans), it was not marketed through Rootes dealers (although all three vehicles were designated as official conversions). The 'D' type retained the same style of hard top as the 'C' but is easily distinguishable by means of the quarterlights fitted to the doors.

The 'D' type Harrington was announced shortly after the introduction of the Series 3 Alpine, which was fitted with the front door quarter lights. (Mark Woodfine)

It is believed that the Harrington in this photo was the only one to be built using the Series 4 Alpine as its base. (Mark Woodfine)

At the time of introduction, Harrington's were being 'leaned on' by the Rootes Group (apparently because of their decision not to use certain Rootes components in their coach and commercial body building department), and it was not long before Thomas Harrington Ltd. was taken over by Robins and Day Ltd., a group of companies controlled by the Rootes family. With the take-over, the coach building departments were promptly closed and production of the 'D' type ceased. It is believed that only a few prototypes were built before the closure. It turned out that Robins and Day Ltd. had been a bit hasty: they were left with a number of hard tops in stock and no likelihood of selling them. They decided to make a few more Harrington 'D' types, presumably for special orders, but production was extremely limited as they no longer had the skilled staff to build them in any quantity. Those that were built were of as high a quality as their predecessors. Just how many were built is anyone's guess. The Sunbeam Alpine Owners Club does know of a Series 4-bodied 'D' type, owned by one of its members, which may possibly be the last Harrington Alpine. Most people agree that there were less 'D' types than 'C' types, which gives some indication as to its rarity.

Anyone considering buying a Harrington should make sure that the car was in fact built by Harrington's. Several 'cowboys' tried to convert standard Alpines by making hard tops to the same design as the Harrington but invariably neglected to fit the necessary strengthening sections to the chassis. I don't need to emphasize how dangerous that can be.

THE SUNBEAM VENEZIA

Most people have probably never heard of this car, and the few that have might well ask what it has got to do with the Sunbeam Alpine. The answer is quite simple – not a lot! – only the way it came about and some of the spare parts used to build it.

To be fair, the majority of the car belongs to the Humber Sceptre Mark 1. But apart from the influence the Alpine played in the Venezia's design, the Venezia is a particular favourite of mine and is the only other vehicle, at present, to be eligible for entry into the S.A.O.C. For these reasons, I believe it deserves some space in this book.

The Venezia is undoubtedly the least known Sunbeam ever built. Those concerned with its design and manufacture have long since disappeared, or are hesitant to give away any secrets, which means that providing a full history of the car is virtually impossible. This is what I managed to find out with the aid of two S.A.O.C. members, Keith Pountain and Peter French, both of whom are Venezia owners.

The Sunbeam Venezia, probably one of the rarest of Rootes Group vehicles, designed and built by Superleggera Touring Milan. The car's aluminium body was fitted to a Humber Sceptre floorpan.

Alec Caine arranged for a great deal of the Alpine's development and subsequent modifications to be carried out by an Italian coachbuilding firm, Carrozia Superleggera Touring Milano. No doubt it was the friendship which had built up between Alec and Superleggera's directors which brought about the Venezia project, together with the fact that Rootes Italia had given Superleggera the contract to build the C.K.D. (kit) Alpines and Super Minxes. As the majority of Alec's Alpine projects were concentrated on finding more space and leg room, the idea of a 'stretched' Alpine with four proper seats appealed to him. Rumours began to circulate in the motoring world that such a car was in the pipeline and that it was to be the replacement for the current Rapier.

The new car was unveiled in September 1963 at St. Marks Square, Venice (hence the name Venezia), after being brought to the square via a somewhat hazardous journey by gondola. It was immediately obvious to the press that the car was way out of the Rapier's price class and was in fact a very smart coachbuilt saloon. They were told that it was to be sold in Italy only, which caused quite an uproar among would-be British buyers. Only about seven Venezias found their way to the U.K. and that included the prototype (now owned by another S.A.O.C. member).

Basically, the Venezia uses the Sceptre's steel floorpan (identical to

The first Venezia was taken to St. Mark's Square, Venice by gondola, for its unveiling. The gent. in the photo was about to regret leaning on the car, as nobody had set the handbrake. (Alec Caine)

The Venezia was sold only in Venice — hence its name.

the Super Minx and Vogue items) to form a semi-rigid base for the new body structure. On to this was built a special thin tubular steel framework to take the unstressed aluminium body panels. The combination of floorpan and tubular cage was enough to give the new body the same strength and rigidity as the Sceptre's pressed steel monocoque structure, while ensuring that the Venezia was 100 lb. lighter.

Take a close look at the bodywork and you can see the Alpine influence in the front and rear wings. The rear wings are chopped as on the modification carried out to Alec's Series 2 Alpine in 1960 (but not introduced until the Series 4). You can also see a grille from the Rapier, and headlights and front windscreen from the Mark 1 Sceptre. It was

91

said that the rear windscreen was a Super-Minx front windscreen, but Mr Pountain has proved this to be false when he tried to fit one to one of the Venezias he is restoring.

Apart from some minor modifications and engine tuning carried out by Superleggera, the Venezia's mechanics are standard Sceptre. The tuning to the 1592 c.c. engine involved gas-flowing the cylinder head, fitting a special camshaft (timings of 29°, 63°, 61°, 31°) and a special distributor to match the camshaft, and fitting tubular steel push rods. This gave 88 b.h.p. net at 5,800 r.p.m.

Small Car summed up this hybrid as follows: 'In fact, what Touring has done is link up a whole shelf full of prestyled bits and pieces with a series of uncomplicated curves to give one of the best looking specials of all times, and whatever you may think of certain details (such as those rearward-sloping centre pillars), that's quite an achievement.'

The exact number of cars built is not known. Records show that only 145 Sceptre floorpans were supplied to Superleggera direct from the U.K. The chassis numbers taken from cars we know of show a top limit of 200 and it is believed that Superleggera converted parts from the C.K.D. Super Minxes to achieve this number. Production ceased early in 1965 when Superleggera began to get into financial difficulties.

When the car was first announced, there were rumours that if it was well received, it would be assembled by Jensen in England and fitted with a Ford V.8 engine, like the Tiger, giving a very fast luxury sports saloon car for introduction into the American market. When Chrysler took over the Rootes Group, they asked Jensen to produce a Venezia with a 4.5 litre Chrysler V.8 unit. Unfortunately, as with so many other projects in the motor industry, all these plans came to nothing.

Sunbeam Venezia: General details

Price:	£1,440 before tax and duty
Top speed:	101 m.p.h.
Acceleration:	0–30 5.3 secs.
(on wet road)	0–40 8.6 secs.
	0–50 13.5 secs.
	0–60 18.4 secs.
	0–70 26.3 secs.
Overall fuel consumption:	25.6 m.p.g.
(under test conditions)	
Length:	177 inches
Width:	62 inches
Height:	54 inches
Weight:	2480 lb.

The Colotti Alpine never actually made production. Only the one prototype was built, incorporating a five-speed gearbox and die cast magnesium wheels, as well as the specially designed hard top. It was originally used by Alf Francis as his personal transport — but where is it now?

The Ashley Organization, renowned for their detachable hard tops, brought out their own version of a hard top for the Alpine. This was detachable and could be fitted to any standard production Alpine of Series 1 or 2. A moulded parcel shelf covered the area from the cockpit to the lower edge of the rear window, and formed the roof of the boot. It is shown here on Charles Eyre-Maunsell's Circuit of Ireland car. (Charles Eyre-Maunsell)

4
Competition

The Alpine made its debut in international events in the 1959 R.A.C. Rally held between 17th and 20th November, only a few months after its initial release. The Rootes group knew that successful sporting achievements sold cars, and that the Alpine, like its Sunbeam predecessors, would be expected to live up to the fine reputation the Sunbeam name had developed over more than half a century. In particular, rally successes played an ever increasing role in the world of car selling, for they proved that the cars were reliable, strong and could withstand almost anything their owners could put them through.

The R.A.C. Rally, with its 131 competitors, started its gruelling 2,000 mile course at Blackpool with some short driving tests on Blackpool Promenade. Two Alpines had been entered, one a works car driven by Ray and Crabtree, and a second entered by the Alan Fraser Racing Team, driven by Fraser and Shenley Price. Whereas a good time for the driving test was 34 seconds, Alan – with what was described as 'clumsy driving' – managed to take 47.2 seconds, a terrible time and not exactly the best way to start a rally of this calibre. His only consolation was that he was not the slowest. After this warming up heat, the cars set off on a fairly easy passage to Marshaw and Settle, and then on to the Yorkshire dales where the real rallying began. Fog on the by-ways and moor roads made conditions hazardous and by the time the cars reached Brough, the Yorkshire dales had taken their toll. Seventeen cars retired and only 34 crews clocked in unpenalized.

From Brough the route took them via Appleby to the Lake District and the famous Hard Knott Pass. The route, as in the Yorkshire dales, was shrouded in fog, and the ever present peril of wandering sheep hampered their way. Hard Knott Pass claimed several victims as expected, but the two Alpines of Ray and Fraser continued their gruesome task. Visibility was poor, being affected every few minutes by thick fog and heavy cloud.

Wrynose Pass was an extremely tight section, in which it was virtually impossible for one competitor to pass another unless the man in front gave way. This tended to hamper the progress of some of the cars but Ray, in the works Alpine, was fortunate. As he gained on J. Casewell's Austin A99, Casewell pulled over to let Ray through, like a true sporting gentleman.

A torrential downpour made conditions appalling for the tests at Charterhall, which included a standing start and a flying finish between pylons. Easy, you may say, but not so easy in the dark! Gregor Grant discovered this when he was rapidly travelling towards the finish and the lights of his Fairthorpe went out. Ray's Alpine came through the tests the better of the two, after losing only one point, and was placed second in the test behind Morgan's Morgan.

There followed a fairly pleasant ride to Kinlochleven and Garve in the Western Scottish Highlands, for the start of the 'Gairloch and back again' tour. There were rumours that fog was expected but the strong wind kept it at bay. However, the temperature soon began to drop, making snow more likely. From here it was tough going over rough terrain. On the high road to Inverness, the cars had difficulty keeping on the road due to gale force winds accompanied by torrential rain, and the occasional flurries of sleet, hail and snow.

After returning to Garve from the Gairloch tour, the planned route took the cars through Tomintoul (the highest point in Great Britain) down a mountain road to Braemar. Some locals were saying that there was heavy snow on the road, making it impassable, while others maintained that everything would be O.K., as it was melting fast. The cars set off along bone-dry roads for several miles. Tomintoul Village was also snow free, and so everyone tore towards the mountain road full of optimism. But then the cars started to encounter snow drifts, which were getting deeper and deeper. What came next was the turning point of the rally: all those minutes that had been lost in earlier stages were nothing compared with the time which was going to be lost now. The road was blocked. The leaders had to turn around, and unfortunately for them inevitably lost the greatest amount of time. Others, who had set off later, saw them coming back up the road and immediately turned round and tried to find another route. Ray was one of a select few who took the very difficult road over

Devil's Elbow to Blairgowrie, while Fraser took what was classed as a very devious route. Nevertheless, both Alpines made the control point.

It was then a straight run to Kinross and on to the Whitburn control. Once over the Kincadrine bridge a number of competitors got lost and could not find the actual control point. The next stop was Lockerbie and then Oulton Park where there was a short race meeting. It was raining heavily and a great number of cars showed their battle scars as they headed down country to Wales, for what was to be the worst section of the rally.

The organizers had certainly picked some of the worst roads (if they could be called roads). Many were no more than cart tracks which traffic used to get to inaccessible places with unpronounceable names such as Llanrhaiadr, Llanuwchllyn and Bwylch-y-Groes. These mostly unusable tracks, including the well known Farmer's Mountain road, led to Eppynt and the regularity test which was in two sections of 3.25 and 4.33 miles, the latter being by far the more difficult.

The South Wales section proved just as arduous as the North Wales section and the roads just as treacherous. The last phase from Treorchy to Talybent was made even more difficult by thick fog, which reduced visibility to next to nil in places. Talybent control proved very hard to find. Someone had deliberately altered the approach sign which caused a great many competitors to miss the control altogether, and then, by having to search for it, lose valuable time and points. Retirements were high. These so called roads had punished the cars beyond the extreme but the two Alpines of Ray and Fraser rolled on and on, through Cheltenham, Prescott, Harleyford, to a quick spin round Brands Hatch racing circuit and so on to the final control at the Crystal Palace racing track. This last phase from Brands to Crystal entailed some really fast motoring to maintain the average speed of 30 m.p.h. which was required. Once they reached the South London traffic, delays were inevitable and Crystal was not the easiest place to get to.

The event closed with a series of five lap races – something which everyone could have done without. Alan Fraser spun his Alpine at Ramp Bend in front of Brian Harper and his Morgan, causing some anxiety for both drivers, but they came out unscathed.

Only 53 out of the 131 starters had finished the course. The two Alpines had been subjected to far more stress than anything the development team could devise, and they had survived. The cars finished third and fifth in class – quite an achievement for their first international event.

The R.A.C. Rally proved that the Alpine could withstand almost anything. This brought a sudden rush of privately entered Alpines for

Mary Handley Page and Pauline Mayman in the 21st International Alpine Rally, 1960. Mary Handley Page spares a hand for a wave on the most dangerous pass of all, the Gavia in the Dolomites.

what is probably the most famous and toughest of all rallies – the Monte Carlo. The 1960 event was the 29th in the series, with 345 starters aiming to cover the 2,350 miles in seven days. Nobody at Rootes expected the Alpine to win outright, due to the ridiculous handicapping system: they would be content if the cars finished. So when Backlund and Falk drove their Swedish entered Alpine to first place in its class, not to mention the five other cups they won, they had surpassed everyone's expectations.

Privately entered Alpines in international competitions came out extremely well and on a number of occasions beat the works-entered cars. One man who achieved this consistently was Charles Eyre-Maunsell, a Rootes dealer in Ireland. Although he rarely raced outside Ireland, he dominated the events he did enter, whether it was on a rally circuit or a race circuit.

The first event he entered was the 1960 International Circuit of Ireland, a 1,500-mile event held between 15th and 19th April 1960. 127 cars

Charles Eyre-Maunsell with his 1960 Circuit of Ireland rally car. He came third in class, after leading the rally until the very last driving test. (Charles Eyre-Maunsell)

started from controls in Belfast, Dublin and Omagh, joining a common route in Dundalk after the Belfast and Omagh starters had crossed into Eire. This first section was straight-forward and free from incident. For the second stage each car was issued with a sheet containing 11 map references, the distance between each two points and the minimum number of minutes allocated to cover the distance. Marks were deducted at the rate of 2 per minute for late arrival at any of these points, with the normal 10 marks per minute operating at the final control. It was obviously not an easy task to complete the course without losing some marks and only 12 cars came through with clean sheets. One of these was Charles in his Alpine. To keep the crews of the cars on their toes, the organizers served up a driving test at the third control, followed by a very long road section with an optional check point. They then headed for Dunmore East for a short hill climb and a 60-minute breakfast in

Tramore. The cars did not even have time to cool down before they set off again, heading westward through a series of driving tests with the end of the first stage in Killarney and a very welcome overnight stop. By then, Charles had built up a very comfortable lead in the large G.T. class, with Armstrong second in an M.G.A. and Parkes third in a Healey 3000.

The next stage consisted of numerous timed points. To say that the pace was hot would be an understatement, judging by the number of bent motors which returned to Killarney that night. This stage also contained a timed descent and a timed ascent of 'Tim Healy Pass'. Charles's Alpine had not proved very manoeuvrable in the tighter driving tests but displayed considerable power on the hills. (He has assured me that all the cars he used over the years were practically standard as far as the mechanics were concerned.)

While the Sprite of Sherry and the V.W. of Boyd led the way downhill, the Alpine came into its own on the way up, with Charles taking third place overall behind the big Healey 3000s of Pat Moss and Parkes. After a further day of manoeuvrability tests and some very rough road sections, the final stage contained three timed laps of the Kirkistown Circuit and three driving tests, one of which was the circuit's famous braking test held before thousands of spectators. After a magnificent display throughout the rest of the event, Charles Eyre-Maunsell waited to start this last section of the rally. He was given the go signal, and with an incredible flying start he dashed through the section faster than any other competitor, coming up the 44 foot channel (through which the cars must average at least 30 m.p.h.) and preparing himself to stop in the shortest distance possible in the pylon-lined curve beyond it. Charles applied the brake and the car headed towards the first of the pylons. It then proceeded to go down the row like the 'Rat-a-tat-tat' of machine gun fire, collecting some 15 pylons each carrying 15 penalty points. This left the class open for Parkes in his Healey 3000. (As a matter of interest, Parkes had the same misfortune during the 1959 rally.) Charles was knocked into third place and the works-entered Alpine of E. T. McMillen came fifth in class.

In the 1961 event Charles lost his first place again, when his distributor jumped clean out of the engine on the second stage. The inevitable delay while he tried to fix it incurred heavy penalties and again he came third in class. He continued to enter the circuit every year up to 1965 but through various misfortunes never managed to better this placing. He regularly entered Alpines at most race track meetings held in Ireland, normally finishing first or second, and in 1962 and 1963 won the Sports Car (points) Championship Trophy.

The Rootes competition department, headed by Norman Garrad, continued to enter the odd Alpine in international rallies, but their main

Charles Eyre-Maunsell driving one of his circuit-racing Alpines in the last race of the 1962 Sports Car Championship, which he won. (Charles Eyre-Maunsell)

Charles Eyre-Maunsell entered most race meetings in Ireland and can be seen here in the Leinster Motor Club Dunboyne Trophy Race, in which he finished third. (Charles Eyre-Maunsell)

concern was with the Rapier which, because of the handicapping system, stood a better chance of winning rallies outright. At the beginning of 1961, they decided to look into the idea of entering works Alpines in track events – after all, it was a sports car. The main problem was that they had not entered international racing events for a number of years, although everyone concerned did have experience of them. Garrad, for instance, was well known at Brooklands for some fine performances with the big Talbots. But times had changed, and team work in the pits on long distance races could win or lose a race. They simply did not have this experience. In early 1961, however, they decided to enter the 1961 Sebring 12-hour race in the U.S.A. The race was to be held on 25th March, and in February Norman Garrad hired Silverstone Grand Prix Circuit to enable his team to practise a few pit stops, while the Alpine

In February 1961, Norman Garrad hired the Silverstone circuit to test out the Alpine before its first international race meeting at Sebring. The photo shows, among others, Raymond Baxter (leaning over), and the two drivers, Peter Harper (in front of Baxter) and Peter Proctor (above Baxter).

Peter Harper (centre) discusses the Alpine's steering qualities with Norman Garrad (right), while Jack Brabham listens in.

The Silverstone testing session was to be an all-night vigil. John Parkes (in white helmet) was the third test driver.

lapped the circuit in a dawn to dusk test to check tyre wear, a vital feature of the Sebring '12 hour'.

Three works Alpines were entered:

Car No. 40 driven by Hopkirk and Jopp;

Car No. 41 driven by Wilson and Tamburo;

Car No. 42 driven by Harper and Proctor.

No one seriously expected them to win the race outright. Even with the greatest will in the world, you cannot expect a straight four-cylinder 1592 c.c. engined Alpine to beat a V.12 Ferrari, but then not everyone goes to these races to see the big cars. Some people prefer to see the cars they can afford battle it out with the 'big fellows', to see how they stand up to the severe punishment meted out on the track. Class 9 was designated for G.T. cars up to 1600 c.c., and as expected this turned out to be quite a battle between the Alpines and the M.G.A.s.

Sebring is an old airfield, utilizing some of the perimeter and main runways as the track. It can certainly give the cars a lot of punishment as well as keeping the drivers on their toes, as they never know what is going to happen next. Peter Harper (who by coincidence had learned to fly at Sebring during the war) described Sebring in his book *Destination Monte*, while talking about the long distance races he had entered: 'Sebring was the most amusing, and certainly I saw some of the worst driving there. Anyone who can afford an expensive sports car, it seems, can take part. The method used by some of the Sebring characters to find the ultimate speed into a corner was to keep taking them faster and faster until eventually they ran off. As there was nothing on the outside of most of the corners, the procedure was simply to motor on until the driver was able to return to the circuit further on.'

As zero hour approached the colourful pageant (usually found at American events) was well under way and the 65 starters were in echelon in front of the pits. The track started to clear when the five minutes warning horn blast was given and Governor Bryant prepared to unfurl the starting flag. At precisely 10 a.m. the flag fell, and they were off – well, most of them. Stirling Moss's Maserati unfortunately had a flat battery and would not start, and he lost 6 minutes getting it changed.

Peter Proctor (car 42) and Paddy Hopkirk (car 40) had by lap four built up a very useful lead in class 9. Then Hopkirk took over the lead from Proctor, their nearest challenger being the Parkinson/Flaherty M.G.A. which had developed what was described as a peculiar high pitched whistle and kept the crowds wondering what was causing it.

After three hours they had proved that there was nothing in class 9 that could catch the Alpine and their lead was getting longer and longer – until they came in for their pit stops. The practice at Silverstone in February had not been sufficient. It took the Rootes crew about 6 minutes for a tyre change and fuel tank refill, whilst it was taking M.G. only 1 minute 20 seconds. This enormous difference was steadily eroding the lead the Alpines had built up in the early stages.

Car 41 dropped out with engine trouble and after four hours the Hopkirk/Jopp car was getting visibly slower. Peter Harper had now taken over the driving of car 42 but soon had to make another pit stop to have the brakes adjusted. While this was being done Parkinson's whistling M.G.A. took over the lead, closely followed by his team mate Riley, now in second place.

Peter Harper rejoined the race and had just started the task of catching up the Abingdon contingent when Paddy Hopkirk's car pulled into the pits with a blown head gasket, which the mechanics set about changing (and that's something you don't see done today!). Peter's fight back was in vain. His brakes were giving him problems and more and more pit stops had to be made, giving the Abingdon cars a chance to build up the lead they needed to stay in front. At one pit stop, Peter Proctor was coming in to change over drivers, and Jim Ashworth, the chief mechanic, stood as usual with his arms outstretched, showing him where to stop. Peter's brakes failed and Jim was deposited in the pit control box.

The M.G.s of Parkinson/Flaherty and Riley/Whitmore finally won the day, with Peter Harper and Peter Proctor's car coming third in class. The Rootes works team had learned the hard way, that time lost in the pits did lose races. This was something they had to practise and practise again, before they could return to put the record straight.

The full list of lap times was never published. Although the placings are believed to be accurate, the timekeepers had a lot of problems and could not agree as to just how many laps each car covered. To everyone's dismay, this was never actually sorted out.

Results of Sebring 12 Hour Endurance Race, 1961

Overall position	Drivers	Car	Laps	Av. speed
1	Hill/Gendebien	Ferrari	210	91.000
2	Von Trips/Ginther	Ferrari	208	90.133
3	P. & R. Rodriguez	Ferrari	207	89.7
4	Sharp/Hissom	Ferrari	202	87.533
5	Holbert/Penske	Porsche	199	86.233
6	Hall/Contantine	Ferrari	197	85.366

7	Donner/Sesslar	Porsche	196	84.933
8	Reed/Sturgis	Ferrari	191	82.766
9	Ryan/Bradley	Porsche	186	80.6
10	McCluggage/Eager	Ferrari	179	77.566
11	Johnson/Morgan	Chevrolet	172	74.533
12	Newman/Publicker	Ferrari	171	74.1
13	Hall/Ross	Lola		
14	Parkinson/Flaherty	MGA		
15	Buzzetta/Carlson	Sebring Sprite		
16	Riley/Whitmore	MGA		
17	Harper/Proctor	Sunbeam Alpine		
18	Helburn/Fulp	Ferrari		
19	Cunningham/Kimberley	Maserati		
20	Peck/Hoffman	Osca		
21	Durbin/Gibson	Arnolt-Bristol		
22	Gates/Rickett	Corvette		
23	Payne/Gary	Arnolt-Bristol		
24	Seaverns/Cuomo	Arnolt-Bristol		
25	Leavens/Colgate	Sebring Sprite		
26	Rogers/Baily	Morgan		
27	Rebeque/Sales	Alfa Romeo		
28	Swanson/Durant	Alfa Romeo		
29	Rushin/Parsons	Triumph TR3		
30	Waltman/Williamson	Triumph TR3		
31	Theodoli/Barrette	Sunbeam Alpine		
32	Yenko/Moore	Corvette		
33	O'Brien/Jacobson	Alfa Romeo		
34	Hopkirk/Jopp	Sunbeam Alpine		
35	Gelder/Dennis	Elva Courier		
36	Horn/Tucker	Elva Courier		
37	Spinzel/Hawkins	Sebring Sprite		

In early 1961, the Royal Scottish Automobile Club had threatened to cancel the International Scottish Rally, because of lack of support. Among the 60 drivers who responded to the club's plea by entering the 1961 event was John Melvin, a Rootes main dealer in Scotland. The rally itself turned out to be very closely fought, with the final result kept hanging in the balance until the very last driving test held on 24th May.

The rally started with some driving tests held at the Gleneagles Hotel on Monday, 22nd May. This was followed by some special stages at Logie

Kirk, the Path of Condie and the notorious Bridge of Balgie. Agnes Mickel in a Sprite took the least time through the Gleneagles test (23.4 seconds). The Path of Condie turned out to be quite an easy section, but the Bridge of Balgie, as expected, really put the cars and drivers through their paces. The Alpine came into its own on the mountainous section and was the first car through, followed by Foden in an Aston Martin D.B.4.

John Melvin took Tuesday's stages with special care as it contained two special untried sections at Glenbreckie (near to the Mull of Kintyre) and the so called Pollinwilune-Davar road among its 250-mile length. This caught out a few competitors and the retirements began to mount, but it caused no problems for John Melvin. Wednesday's tests at Connel Ferry started off with the famous dash and wiggle test, in which a standing start $\frac{1}{2}$-mile straight section leads directly to a series of manoeuvring tests and a slalom. The Aston Martin D.B.4 gained Foden a few extra marks, reaching 120 m.p.h. (or so it was claimed) before he braked for the first pylon. Foden naturally won the test, but John Melvin also had a very good run and picked up a few marks through sheer speed.

This was followed by a further two driving tests and a section of 103 miles which led to Monument Hill at Dalmally, for a hill climb/special section. For most of the competitors, this was a chance to try to sharpen up on the climb, for the course was exactly the same as on the R.A.C. Rally. The road was rough and dusty and conditions were reported to be very similar to those on an Alpine Rally special section. John Melvin's Alpine sailed through, making the fastest time and winning the section.

On Thursday morning, it was announced that John Melvin had taken the lead, with the Mickel Sprite in second place. The overnight rain gave the leaders something to think about at the 'Little Rest' where yet another driving test was held. John's Alpine was a bit too responsive when he accelerated, nearly losing time through wheelspin which would have jeopardized his lead. At the 'Rest and be thankful' section, Awton's Triumph came out on top, beating John by just one second. This was followed by some very easy road sections which marked the end of the rally.

John Melvin and his Alpine had won the rally outright. The car was fast and handled well, surprising many people by the speed it attained in some of the tests. In fact, prior to the rally, John had removed the engine and sent it to the Rootes works competition department for race tuning. They duly returned an engine to him, which he fitted into the car. Due to lack of time, he could give it no more than a few short road tests before entering the rally. To John's surprise, when he returned home he found a note apologizing for a mistake. The works had sent him a brand new standard engine. Throughout the rally John had been putting the car's speed down

The two Le Mans cars just before they were taken to the race track. The photo shows the four drivers — (from left to right) Peter Jupp, Paddy Hopkirk, Peter Proctor and Peter Harper — and Norman Garrad, Rootes' competition manager, shaking hands with the garage proprietor.

to the works' preparation, and now he found he had won the rally using a completely standard car. He was amazed – and so was the works!

Probably the most famous of the Alpine's successes was winning the 'Index of Thermal Efficiency' at the 1961 Le Mans. After the Sebring fiasco, the works team mechanics practised their pit stop procedure over and over again until they had mastered the art. This team consisted of Norman Garrad (manager), Jim Ashworth (foreman), and mechanics, Gerry Spencer, Jack Walton, Ernie Beck, George Cole, Dick Wright, Johnny Butcher and Bill Knight. Two Alpines were entered: a completely standard model (reg. 3001 RW) driven by Hopkirk and Jopp, and the Harrington Le Mans (reg. 3000 RW), driven by Harper and Proctor.

Although the race itself started at 4 p.m. on 10th June 1961, it started

After scrutineering, the engine seals are fixed on the Harrington Alpine.

for the team at 7 a.m. on Tuesday, 6th June, with the scrutineering, which was held for the first time in the new scrutineering enclosure out on the circuit. The new enclosure had been equipped with a hoist, weighbridge and other amenities which allowed the scrutineering to be carried out more accurately and quickly. Each car had to pass through a long line of verification posts, at each of which some aspect was examined, such as engine details, body dimensions, suspension and so on. All went well until the two Alpines came to the ground clearance check, where they were rolled over a large thin rectangular wooden box placed on a level section of concrete. This was to ensure that the cars' ground clearance was sufficient to meet current regulations. Unfortunately, as so often happened, there was a horrible grating noise from underneath, indicating that the cars had grounded on the box. Everyone dropped onto his knees to look underneath and see which part of the cars' anatomy was causing the difficulty. In the case of both Alpines, it was the undershield which had been fitted to reduce drag. At first everyone thought they would have to be removed, but I have been assured that they were not. Nobody could tell me how they overcame the problem, but I suspect that they pumped more air into the tyres until the cars cleared the box. This was the method used by most racing teams faced with that sort of problem.

The practice sessions took place between 7 p.m. and 11 p.m. on Wednesday, 7th June and part of the following Thursday. They were remarkably incident-free but were marred by a blazing row between the drivers of the works cars and Norman Garrad. He insisted that the drivers should arrive at the track at 10 a.m. on the day of the race, 10th June (there was no practising on the 9th), when it didn't actually start until 4 p.m. Everyone but Norman thought this an unnecessary waste of nervous energy, but he wanted to keep a personal eye on everything and everyone. As the man in charge of the whole venture, he must have had quite a responsibility to his team and his company.

At 4 p.m. precisely Monsieur Panhard raised the starting flag high and then swept it to the ground, and the 1961 Le Mans 24-hour Grand Prix D'Endurance race was on. The Sunbeams, making their first appearance

At 4 p.m. precisely, the race started with the usual melée to grab a piece of the track.

The Harper–Proctor car circled the track with complete regularity, only stopping to change drivers and take on fuel.

at Le Mans for 36 years, were to have an almost totally uneventful race. The Harrington ran perfectly, giving no problems at all. The standard Alpine of Hopkirk and Jopp (3001 RW) was by far the quicker of the two but unfortunately, due to a misunderstanding in the pits, it was disqualified at 0402 hours after 130 laps, for replenishing the gearbox oil too soon.

The Harper/Proctor car continued steadily and unobtrusively with complete regularity, only stopping to take on fuel and oil. The drivers had decided to drive in stints of three hours, as they found that this was sufficient to stop fatigue. The last three hours were the worst by far, for the brakes had almost gone and there was little tread left on the tyres. After 24 hours of continuous driving, they had achieved the impossible: they had won the 'Index of Thermal Efficiency'. This forbidding title simply designates the car that runs in the most efficient way throughout the race. It is calculated on the weight of the car, the petrol used, and the average speed over the 24 hours. To every motorist it is, in fact, of greater significance than the championship itself. The organizers obviously realized this, giving £2,250 for the index title compared with £3,750 for the outright winner (a Ferrari which was in effect a racing car with two seats and of little use to the general public).

To everyone's amazement, Harper and Proctor's Harrington Alpine won the Index of Thermal Efficiency.

All the competitors in the race had been given a thermal efficiency target but as the race had been run at such a hot pace only a handful of cars could reach their figure. The pale green Alpine was one of the select few. Superbly driven by Peter Proctor and Peter Harper, and backed by one of the slickest pit crews on the track, under the guidance of Norman Garrad, the Alpine covered a total distance of 2,180 miles, using only 122.5 gallons of petrol. This gave a consumption of 18 miles per gallon, a tremendous figure, bearing in mind the fact that the car averaged over 91 m.p.h. with a fastest lap of 95.5 m.p.h. and was timed down the Mulsanne straight at over 115 m.p.h.

The Alpine's success was due to 100 per cent reliability. Apart from refuelling and cleaning the windscreen, the pit crews had had very little to do. They did not even change the tyres. During the whole race the car had spent less than nine minutes in the pits, which just failed to beat the existing record. It was a fitting reward for the many hours of practice the team had put in since the Sebring escapade.

Le Mans 24 Hours, 1961: Hour by Hour Positions

Hours:	2	3	4	5	6	7	8	9	10	11	12
3000 RW	38	34	34	31	31	28	30	29	27	27	24
3001 RW	37	32	31	30	27	25	27	27	26	24	

Hours:	13	14	15	16	17	18	19	20	21	22	23	24
3000 RW	20	21	23	22	21	21	18	21	21	21	17	16

Le Mans 24 Hours, 1961: How They Finished

Overall positions	Car	Cubic capacity	Laps	Av. speed
1	Ferrari	2953	2782.2	115.925
2	Ferrari	2953	2758.6	114.941
3	Ferrari	2953	2646.4	110.266
4	Maserati	2984	2599.1	108.295
5	Porsche	1967	2582.0	107.583
6	Ferrari	2953	2579.4	107.475
7	Porsche	1606	2559.9	106.662
8	Maserati	1989	2528.7	105.362
9	Triumph	1985	2371.8	98.825
10	Porsche	1588	2371.4	98.808
11	Triumph	1985	2330.7	97.112
12	Lotus	1216	2233.5	93.062
13	Lotus	1216	2229.7	92.904
14	Fiat Abarth	847	2193.3	91.387
15	Triumph	1985	2188.5	91.187
16	Sunbeam Alpine	1592	2182.2	90.925
17	AC Bristol	1971	2178.0	90.75
18	DB Panhard	702	2124.3	88.512
19	DB Panhard	850	2031.3	84.637
20	DB Panhard	850	2031.2	84.633
21	DB Panhard	850	1997.8	83.241
22	DB Panhard	850	1981.2	82.55

The Alpine had been having tremendous success on the United States circuits and was currently leading its class in the 1961 S.C.C.A. Championship, as well as thrashing much larger-engined cars in other

our cups runneth over

We hoped to let you know what a winning breed of competition car Sunbeam Alpine is by putting all the trophies it has won into the car and taking a picture.

But, as we have said, our cups runneth over—even with the windows rolled up. Frankly, we were surprised. Our Alpine is an extremely roomy car. It has big, deep-cushioned seats, six-footer leg room, an accommodating rear seat for children or parcels, extra-wide lockable doors, too. Yet Sunbeam Alpine will not hold all the trophies it has won in only 3 years of proving itself against any and all comers. Over 163 awards—and the record is not complete.

We're particularly proud of Alpine's 1st at the Le Mans 24-hour Grand Prix; an average of 91 mph for 2194 miles, at 18 miles to the gallon, for the Index of Thermal Efficiency Cup. And at the Riverside (Cal.) Grand Prix, where Alpine bested D, E and G, and all Class F entries.

Sunbeam Alpine, track champion, superlative road car, and only $2595 p.o.e.* Our cups—indeed, our cup—runneth over.

SUNBEAM ALPINE

*East P.O.E. Slightly more in west. State & local taxes, delivery charge, if any, hard top, wire wheels, white walls optional, extra.   Going abroad? Ask your Rootes dealer about our overseas delivery plan.

A BETTER BUY BECAUSE IT'S BETTER BUILT BY **ROOTES** MAKERS OF HILLMAN / SUNBEAM / SINGER / HUMBER

classes. This prompted Jack Brabham's racing organization (who were now marketing tuning kits for the Alpine) to enter an Alpine in the three-hour Grand Prix D'Endurance held at Riverside near Los Angeles. This is an artificial road circuit with a fairly long straight and plenty of twists and turns. Couple this with the length and speed of this race and you have an ideal situation in which to test both driver and car.

The Alpine was not one of Jack Brabham's own cars, but was American owned and prepared, and not particularly well prepared at that. Too stiff an anti-roll bar had been fitted which gave the car a tendency to understeer. This could have been fixed easily if they had had time, but Jack arrived at the race track with only enough time to have a short practice session and do a few minor adjustments to the engine. As a result, the Alpine lost a couple of seconds a lap throughout the race. Even so, it managed to see off everything in its class and indeed most of the cars in all the other classes, which included a very formidable list of vehicles.

Stirling Moss was without a car for this race and he teamed up with Jack Brabham to drive the Alpine. Jack described the start in a magazine article: 'I'll never forget the traffic jam after the starter dropped the flag. It was something like piling through Piccadilly at a hundred miles an hour.

Jack Brabham's organization entered an American-prepared Alpine for the Riverside 3-hour Endurance Race. As Stirling Moss had no car for this race, Jack invited him to drive the Alpine for the last hour.

It seems that American race-goers had a free hand as to how they prepared their cars, unlike their British counterparts. The photo shows Jack Brabham in his Alpine, with the windscreen removed — something that would not have been allowed in the U.K.

The crush was so great that it was quite terrifying for the first few laps. There were cars everywhere – on the course, off the course, up the banks, and bumping one another like dodgems on a fairground.'

He managed to keep clear of trouble and settled down to a comfortable drive, with the engine roaring away healthily and never missing a beat. He gave it quite a bit of stick, getting up to 108 m.p.h. on the main straight. Jack drove for the first two hours and then let Stirling take over. The Alpine showed up particularly well going up the hill and through the esses – the trickiest part of the course – where it was able to gain on almost every other machine in the race.

Stirling held on to the class lead and kept ahead of many other much larger-engined cars. Towards the end of the race he managed to catch up the car that was running in third place overall; waiting for his chance, he took him with his customary brilliance.

The final results was a class win and an incredible third place overall. The car had covered 225 miles in 69 laps at an average speed of 75 m.p.h. They discovered later that they might have gone quite a bit quicker had

The Brabham/Moss Alpine came first in its class and third overall, beating numerous much larger-engined Chevrolets and the like.

they not miscalculated the amount of fuel they carried. They still had over half a tank of petrol left at the end of the race.

The day was not without incident, as the organizers proceeded to announce that the Alpine had finished 6th in class. At this, Jack, Stirling and Norman Garrad – armed with his own detailed lap chart – stormed off to see the timekeepers. Eventually they agreed they had made a mistake and announced the correct results. This brought a flurry of protest from the losers who claimed that the Alpine's fuel tank was bigger than that in the production model. Norman quickly proved that the long distance tank could be bought over the counter and the protests were squashed.

In the 15 years Jack Brabham had been racing, this was the first time he had competed in any production sports car race. He was glad of the experience, saying 'I found it a very comfortable way to go motor racing. I enjoyed myself so much I think I'd like to have another go.' This he did, and he was often to be seen in his Alpine at various circuits throughout the States and the U.K.

Now that the works mechanics had mastered the art of pit team work, they decided to set off once more for the Sebring 12-hour race. This time they were confident that they could give the well respected Abingdon

3001 RW went straight into rallying after the Le Mans race. It is shown here in the 1962 Monte Carlo Rally, driven by Gregor Grant and C. Davis.

Another 1962 Monte Carlo Alpine, driven by Rossdale and Freeman. Like the other two Alpines entered in the rally, it completed the gruelling course.

Notwithstanding the disastrous 1961 Sebring race, Rootes competition department sent another three Alpines to the U.S.A. in 1962, to continue their battle with the Abingdon contingent.

contingent a good run for their money. They knew that the competition was going to be stiff as several more makes of car had entered their class, including Porsche and T.V.R. Porsche would without a doubt cause the biggest problems: if they went the distance, the Sunbeam's chance of winning their class would be slim. T.V.R. had also started to build up quite a reputation and could not be dismissed easily, although anything could happen in 12 hours.

Four Sunbeams were entered this year – three standard hard top Alpines and one Harrington 'A' type (car 44):

Car 41 driven by Harper and Proctor;
Car 42 driven by Payne and Sheppard;
Car 43 driven by Miles and Spencer;
Car 44 driven by Theodolio and Barrette.

After the Le Mans type start, the 65 cars scrambled to claim a piece of the track, and there was still a tremendous amount of weaving and charging as they came down the back straight behind the pits on the first lap. Peter Harper had agreed to drive car 41 for the first two hours and described what happened next: 'We were approaching the 180° right hand bend

The three works Alpines driving up to the pits for the start of the 1962 Sebring Endurance Race. They were joined by a fourth Alpine, entered privately by two Americans, Theodolio and Barrette.

On the first lap, Peter Harper, driving car 41, was pushed off the track by a 15-ton juggernaut laughingly called a sportscar (a Chevrolet Corvette Stingray). He went on to beat the M.G.s and the Corvette for good measure.

after the long straight, when an American gentleman (Yenko), driving a well upholstered commercial vehicle, laughingly described as a sports car (Corvette), greeted me sideways on as we entered the bend and pushed me right off the track.

'I spent a very worried three or four laps as I did not know if the bodywork was fouling the tyres or not. As it turned out the only damage was to the bodywork. It said a lot for the strength of the car that it could stop a fifteen ton juggernaut! Later Yenko came over to apologize and told me that if I had not been there to stop him he would have reached Sebring (town) – his brakes had failed to work. I told him it was O.K. but asked him please not to do it again, because it frightened me.'

Both cars continued the race, although the Corvette had definitely come off the worst, being described in *Autosport* as 'sadly tattered at the front with most of the nearside wing having vanished'.

Peter Harper soon caught up to and overtook Ken Miles, who had been leading the other two Alpines, and started the battle which was to last the entire race, between the Sunbeams, M.G.s and the T.V.R.s. This type of British rivalry always led to an especially exciting race.

On lap 2, Parkinson in an M.G.A., was leading Cuomo in a T.V.R., with

The new-style long-distance tanks, with the large filling necks set in the rear window, dramatically reduced the time spent refuelling.

Peter Harper close on their tails, followed by the remainder of the Alpines in a line broken only by another T.V.R. By lap 8 Cuomo had passed Parkinson but Peter Harper was still with them, biding his time. The race had only just started, after all, and twelve hours was a long time. He decided that he might as well let them set the pace as he knew he had the power to stay with them, no matter what they did.

As the battle continued, Peter took Parkinson for a change of scenery and was now sitting on the tail of Cuomo, with Bolton in another T.V.R. just as closely behind. Ken Miles then side-swiped the McCluggage/Eager Osca and unfortunately knocked it out of the race. The pace of the race was tremendous and the Abingdon gents began to realize that they were not going to have it their own way this year. Trying to keep up with the Alpines and T.V.R.s was giving them problems in the engine temperature department.

Peter Proctor took over from Peter Harper and started to put the pressure on Cuomo and his very fast T.V.R. – so much pressure, in fact, that within a short time the T.V.R. came to a halt with irreparable engine damage. This left Peter in front of all his British rivals but sitting in third place in class behind the two untouchable Porsches of Gurney and Barth. They were at this time respectively 6 and 3 laps ahead of him, an unapproachable distance in a race like this. Peter had to be content to stay ahead of the chasing T.V.R. of Donohue and the three works M.G.A.s which they had now lapped.

As the race progressed, the Alpine and T.V.R. stayed in close company. With a couple of hours to go, Donohue challenged his rival, but it came to nothing when a steering arm of his T.V.R. came adrift. The T.V.R. team, led by Ken Richardson, set about repairing it, but by the time the car rejoined the race the Alpine had lapped the circuit many times. This left the Alpine with no serious challenger in its class, while the only other British car that was in front of it was the Cunningham/Flitch Jaguar 'E' type in Class 13. For obvious reasons, the 'E' type had not been part of the previous rivalry, but it could well have been. The gap between it and the Alpine was closing at a considerable rate, which must have been quite embarrassing for the Jaguar team. In fact, the crew made no attempt to get a good placing within the overall rating, which the car was certainly capable of, but instead were content to finish the race and take a class win (which was inevitable as it was the only car in its class).

Joe Sheppard's Alpine had now developed a metallic clatter in the engine department. When he pulled into the pits, Jim Ashworth found a large hole in the crankcase. He told Joe to carry on and finish, as nothing much worse could happen.

37 cars finally finished the race. The Alpine of Harper and Proctor

Only one Alpine failed to finish the race — car 43, driven by Miles and Spencer. Car 42 only just finished, after blowing a rather large hole in the cylinder block.

remained third in class behind the two Porsches, and was placed 15th in the overall rating. It left behind it an impressive list of much larger engined cars, and that included Yenko's Chevrolet, the car that had hit the Alpine on the first lap.

Results of Sebring 12 Hours Endurance Race, 1962

Overall position	Drivers	Car	Laps	Av. speed
1	Bonnier/Bianchi	Ferrari	206	89.142
2	Hill/Gendebien	Ferrari	196	84.933
3	Jennings/Rand	Porsche	195	84.5
4	Serena/Hamil	Ferrari	190	82.333

5	McLaren/Penske	Cooper-Maserati	190	82.333
6	Sharpe/Hissom	Chaparral	189	81.9
7	Gurney/Holbert	Porsche	188	81.466
8	Hugus/Reed	Ferrari	187	81.033
9	Barth/Strahle	Porsche	182	78.866
10	Guichet/Thiele	Abarth	180	78.000
11	Durant/Swanson	Alfa-Romeo	178	77.133
12	Dipriolo/Facetti	Alfa Romeo	178	77.133
13	Ryan/Fulp	Ferrari	176	76.266
14	Cunningham/Fitch	Jaguar	176	76.266
15	Harper/Proctor	Sunbeam Alpine	173	74.966
16	Sears/Hedges	M.G.A.	172	74.533
17	Parkinson/Flaherty	M.G.A.	171	74.1
18	Black/Wyllie	Chevrolet	171	74.1
19	Yenko/Lowther	Chevrolet	169	73.233
20	Whitmore/Olthoff	M.G.A.	169	73.233
21	Johnson/Morgan	Chevrolet	169	73.233
22	Di Priolo/Theodora	Alfa Romeo	168	72.8
23	Bentley/Gordon	Osca	167	72.366
24	Corrigan/Coleman	Porsche	165	71.5
25	Donohue/Signore	T.V.R.	163	70.633
26	Heimrath/Polivka	Porsche	158	68.466
27	Hanna/Toland	D.B.	158	68.466
28	Manley/Newcomer	D.B.	157	68.033
29	Davis/Pulver	Lotus	155	67.166
30	Waltman/Cone	Triumph	154	66.733
31	Fuller/Washburn	Chevrolet	153	66.3
32	Payne/Sheppard	Sunbeam Alpine	151	65.433
33	Theodoli/Barrette	Sunbeam Alpine	150	65.0
34	Dietrich/Haas	Ferrari	147	63.7
35	Rogers/Bailey	Morgan	143	61.966
36	Maggiacomo/Panch	Ford	107	46.366
37	Richards/Kolb	Alfa Romeo	101	43.766

Alpines returned to Sebring for the last time in 1963 with two cars, the first driven by Titus/Adams/Jordan and the second by Theolodi/Kneeland/Barrette. Although not making as good an overall placing as the Harper/Proctor car in 1962, they still managed to get third and fourth place in their class. T.V.R. entered three cars, while M.G. had brought in two of their new larger-engined M.G.B. models. None of these gave the Alpine any cause for concern. All three T.V.R.s dropped out

Paul and Alfonso Romero celebrate their first attempt at the Mexico Rally in their Sunbeam Alpine in 1962: they won it outright.

within 41 minutes of the start and they were quickly followed by the M.G.B.s, whose engines packed up. This was unfortunate as it could have turned out to be quite a good scrap. The race was a lot quicker than in previous years and the Alpine's reliability was proved once again.

Results of Sebring 12 Hours Endurance Race, 1963

Overall position	Drivers (first two only)	Car	Laps	Av. speed
1	Surtees/Scarfiotti	Ferrari 3 ltr.	209	90.567
2	Mairesse/Vaccarella	Ferrari 3 ltr.	208	90.133
3	Rodriguez/Hill	Ferrari 4 ltr.	207	89.7
4	Penskey/Rabst	Ferrari 3 ltr.	203	87.966
5	Abate/Bordeu	Ferrari 3 ltr.	196	84.933
6	Ginther/Ireland	Ferrari 3 ltr.	196	84.933
7	Leslie/Morrill	Jaguar XKE	195	84.5

8	McLaren/Hansgen	Jaguar XKE	194	84.066
9	Holbert/Wester	Porsche Abarth	193	83.633
10	Barth/Linge	Porsche Abarth	193	83.633
11	Hill/Spencer	Shelby A.C. Cobra	192	83.2
12	Olthoff/Bucknum	Austin Healey	187	81.033
13	Bonnier/Cannon	Ferrari 3 ltr.	186	80.5
14	Piper/Cantrell	Ferrari 3 ltr.	186	80.5
15	Sesslar/Cassel	Porsche Abarth	185	80.166
16	Morgan/Johnson	Corvette	182	78.866
17	Robertson/Allen	Corvette	181	78.433
18	Grossman/Thiem	Ferrari 3 ltr.	179	77.566
19	Richards/Kimberley	Jaguar XKE	177	76.7
20	Merino/Rosales	Porsche Abarth	176	76.266
21	Spychiger/Lugano	Simca Abarth	173	74.966
22	Bolton/Rothschild	Triumph T.R.4	172	74.533
23	Riley/Cone	Volvo P1800	170	73.666
24	Gates/Cole	Triumph T.R.4	168	72.8
25	Hopkirk/Morley	Austin Healey	166	71.933
26	Wilson/Tweedale	Triumph Twin Cam	165	71.5
27	McNeil/Clarens	Morgan 2.2	164	71.066
28	Gurney/Spencer	Shelby A.C. Cobra	163	70.633
29	Durant/Swanson	Alfa Romeo	163	70.633
30	Titus/Adams	Sunbeam Alpine	162	70.2
31	Wameron/Lerch	Simca Abarth	160	69.333
32	Tullius/Kellner	Triumph T.R.4	158	68.466
33	Theolodi/Kneeland	Sunbeam Alpine	155	67.166
34	Waltman	Triumph T.R.4	154	66.733
35	Bentley/Gordon	Lotus Elite	151	65.433
36	Lilley/Graham	Lotus Elite	149	64.566
37	Flemming/Badman	Osca	139	60.233
38	Jopp/Maggiacomo	Shelby A.C. Cobra	117	50.7
39	Grant/Campbell	Corvette	46	19.933

Unlike the works cars that entered the European rallies and races such as Le Mans, the cars that were prepared and sent to America for Sebring stayed in the U.S.A. and were sold off immediately after the race. The European event cars returned to the factory where they were completely stripped to the bare shell and rebuilt with meticulous precision, to be used over and over again. This policy became even more pronounced from 1962, when the money available to the competition department was restricted.

One of the works Le Mans cars and two Harringtons were entered in the 1962 R.A.C. Rally. Both Harringtons retired with a split petrol tank, the one shown in the photo being driven by Grant and Pilsworth.

The works were willing to have a go at preparing Alpines for any of the international rallies. Although the suspension of the Le Mans cars made handling very difficult, their power was useful on some of the smoother sections, as is shown here, during the 1963 Tulip Rally.

The 1962 Le Mans Alpines were given a restyled rear end to improve aerodynamics. As the photo shows, they looked remarkably like the T.R.6 produced many years later.

At the beginning of 1962 the department aquired another three Alpines, with the registration numbers 9201 RW, 9202 RW, and 9203 RW. As usual, the cars were stripped and the majority of panels were replaced with specially made aluminium parts. The engines were race prepared and the suspension uprated (with the 1962 Le Mans in mind).

The bodywork came in for some modification, but not to the extent of the Harrington of 1961. This time the profile stayed the same as on the stardard production car. But the boot lid was raised to the level of the fin, giving a squared off effect to the rear of the car to reduce drag. Surprisingly, it gave the car a very good look and would with a few other slight modifications be a very marketable design even today. No doubt this is why Triumph and Jensen-Healey used the idea in their production cars.

Only two of the cars were used at Le Mans in 1962:

Car no. 32 – 9202 RW, driven by Peter Harper and Peter Proctor;

Car no. 33 – 9203 RW, driven by Paddy Hopkirk and Peter Jopp.

These cars turned out to be quite a bit faster than the 1961 Alpines and although they did not win the index, they had a fairly successful race.

The going was not as smooth and easy going as in 1961, but this was perhaps because they were trying to get too much power out of the small engine, which was never designed for the 120-plus m.p.h. top speed they maintained.

Both cars suffered badly from sticking throttles. Apart from this mechanical set back, there was one other incident that Peter Harper remembers well: 'I had one lively moment when approaching White House – a right and then a left hand bend which we could take at around

Again, only two Alpines were entered for the 1962 Le Mans. As the photo shows, they obtained quite a high starting position on the grid, when compared to the larger-engined cars behind them.

110 m.p.h. It had begun to rain and as I approached the bend I noticed a large car coming up behind me. I didn't think he would catch me before the corner so I moved over to the left, ready to take the right hand bend. I sensed as I started to go into the immediate left-hand bend that the car on my tail was attempting to come up on my inside. I tried to take the corner a little wider than usual, to leave room for him if he insisted on going through, but this put me slightly on the wrong side of the camber and the back end of the car went out of control. I'm not certain just how far I travelled up the road sideways, but when I did eventually come out of the slide I came out so fast that I immediately went into a slide the other way. When I eventually got it all sorted out Graham Hill came by laughing his head off, having had a grandstand view of my entertaining half pirouettes.'

At 5.35 a.m. Paddy's car pulled into the pits with bearing problems and the mechanics set about changing them. He rejoined the race at 6.20 a.m. The mechanics put the failure down to the over-revving caused by the sticking throttle and this was confirmed when, shortly after Paddy left the pits, Peter Harper drove in with the same trouble. This had lost them a

Although in more or less standard form, especially when compared to the Harrington entered the previous year, the two Alpines turned out to be about 10 m.p.h. faster. This photo reveals that the suspension was strengthened considerably, as the corner is being taken at about 110 m.p.h.

The extra speed interfered with the Alpines' fuel consumption and although both cars finished the race — an achievement in itself — they failed to win the Index of Thermal Efficiency.

considerable amount of time which lessened their hopes of winning the index. Peter was less fortunate than Paddy: after the new bearings were fitted, he had to join the race for only six laps and then return to the pits to top up the oil, as the car had been inside its minimum re-oiling distance. This lost even more time. At around 10 a.m., the Hopkirk/Jopp car retired with more engine trouble. The remaining Alpine of Harper and Proctor continued, but alas not without its own problems. The overdrive had gone, slowing the car down considerably, while the second and third gears required holding in. They managed to finish the 24 hours and were placed 15th overall, only 18 out of the 55 starters actually completing the race. When you look at the race results you begin to wonder just how far up the field the Alpine would have finished had it not lost nearly an hour in the pits. To finish the race under these conditions was an achievement in itself.

Le Mans 24 Hours, 1962: How They Finished

Overall position	Car	Cubic capacity	Laps	Av. speed	Fastest timed speed along Mulsanne straight
1	Ferrari	3968	331	115.24	171
2	Ferrari	2953	326	113.51	163
3	Ferrari	2953	311	109.10	158
4	Jaguar	3781	310	107.87	
5	Jaguar	3781	310	107.79	168
6	Ferrari	2969	297	103.50	168
7	Porsche	1590	287	100.90	144
8	Lotus Elite	1216	286	99.60	129
9	Ferrari	2953	281	97.85	155
10	Alfa Romeo	1290	281	97.73	135
11	Lotus Elite	1216	278	96.66	132
12	Porsche	1590	272	94.65	140
13	Morgan	1911	270	93.96	127
14	Abarth Simca	1288	268	93.29	130
15	Sunbeam Alpine	1590	268	93.24	118
16	Panhard C.D.	702	255	88.73	118
17	Rene Bonnet	996	255	88.59	123
18	Rene Bonnet	706	253	87.95	110

The team learned a lot at Le Mans. They were surprised at just how much difference blowing up the tyres to 60 lb. all round (less tyre friction

Peter Proctor practising for the 1963 Le Mans.

resistance) or removing a spot lamp (less wind resistance) could really make. As the lap time is largely governed by the speed that can be attained going down the long Mulsanne Straight, slip streaming can make an astonishing difference at Le Mans. As Peter Harper explained, 'As you are travelling down the straight, watching your rev counter, someone passes you slowly. Immediately you tuck in behind, the revs climb. Even if a faster car passes you at 160 m.p.h. and you are doing 120 m.p.h., it still pays to nip in behind. When driving a small car at Le Mans, I'll follow anything from a pheasant to a Ferrari.' Strangely enough, he also found that when a small car tucked in behind him, really close to within a foot or so, the speed of his car increased.

9203 RW never returned to Le Mans but was eventually sold to the Alan Fraser Racing Organization. It was used on circuits throughout the U.K. until it crashed at one event. It was never rebuilt, but was put under cover and left. Only recently it turned up in Dorset and its new owner (an S.A.O.C. member) is now busy restoring it to its former glory.

The third year at Le Mans got off to a disastrous start after an engine blew up in practice. Two Alpines were entered: 9201 RW (33), driven by the now very experienced Le Mans team of Peter Harper and Peter Proctor, and 9202 RW (32), driven by a new crew to the Sunbeam, Lewis

The 1963 Le Mans turned out to be a disastrous race for Sunbeams, as both the Alpines failed to finish. The works team mechanics again managed to get more power from the small engines, and this could well be the reason why they broke down.

and Ballisat. Both failed to finish the race. Car 33 had been averaging 95 m.p.h. when it blew a cylinder head gasket after just six hours of racing. Car 32 retired after 18 hours with a broken crankshaft. At that point, it was leading the 'up to 2 litre G.T. class' at an incredible average speed of 97 m.p.h., despite the fact that it had been without an overdrive for nearly 12 hours (and at Le Mans the overdrive was an essential part of the Alpine's equipment).

During the period from late 1963 to early 1964, the Alpine and its sister car, the Rapier, were gradually phased out of the works team to make way for the two new Rootes models – the Sunbeam Tiger and the Hillman Imp. But this by no means signified the end of the Alpine in competition. It still dominated the race tracks in the U.S.A. and U.K. as well as those of many other countries. For instance, in Canada it could be seen competing in Mosport events up until 1978, when it was still managing to come away with class wins. In the U.K. the most successful Alpine in club events was that belonging to Bernard Unett – XRW 302, one of the original prototypes. In 1964, Bernard decided to enter as a challenger for the Freddie Dixon Challenge Trophy, which was then considered the biggest prize in club racing. The trophy was awarded on a points system, as in Grand Prix racing, worked out on the results of eleven set races. Bernard's one win, five seconds, two thirds and one fourth place were sufficient for him to win the trophy.

At that time, Bernard was a development engineer at Rootes and he got two of his colleagues to help him prepare the car – Peter Coleman and Frederick Evans. They used a special camshaft which had been made in

After each race, the cars were stripped down completely and scrupulously examined before being rebuilt.

Gregor Grant, then editor of Autosport, *regularly borrowed works Alpines, as this allowed him to write an on-the-spot report for his magazine while competing himself. He is shown here in the 1963 Monte Carlo Rally.*

Bernard Unett, the well-known race and rally driver, probably entered more races with his Alpine than any other driver in the U.K. In 1964, he won the Freddy Dixon Trophy. (Bernard Unett)

Sweden. Its squared-topped cam follower lobes gave the engine an extra 10 b.h.p. and made it incredibly fast – so fast that it always caused a few comments from motoring journalists of that time and kept them wondering about what he actually had under the bonnet. The car was basically a shell with an engine (to make it lighter). It was driven to all the race meetings and driven home afterwards, where it doubled up as family transport. In fact, Bernard is adamant that his wife, Joan, used it to do the shopping!

In the U.S.A. (as in Canada), Alpines regularly competed on the race track for a number of years. In 1964 Don Sesslar was first in class 'F' of the S.C.C.A. National Championships. Michael Reed came first in the

The car he used was a prototype Series 1, which kept many people guessing as to why it was so fast. Its secret was a square lobed camshaft, specially made in Sweden. (Bernard Unett)

When the car was not racing, it was used by his wife to go shopping.
(Bernard Unett)

Alan Fraser was another regular Alpine racer. This photo shows one of
his Harrington Le Mans cars, written off after a crash at St. Mary's corner
on the Goodwood racing circuit. (Bernard Unett)

The Alpine dominated the American tracks, winning the Sports Car Club
of America Championship and boosting sales to take the Alpine to the top
of the league for imported cars.

Some of the American Alpines were renowned for their speed. They regularly beat cars of their own class and normally ended up with an overall placing.

1,500–2,000 c.c. class in the Panama Grand Prix in November 1964, and also achieved third place overall. Dan Carmichael and Al Coftner took first and second places in their class at the 1965 Danville Virginia National Races, while Miss R. Smith and Miss Drolet won the ladies' award at the 1966 Daytona 24-hour race. And the list goes on and on.

And so the story ends. I have refrained from describing the Alpine's successes in normal club events, as the list of these is almost endless. Although I have records of literally hundreds, they are by no means complete. Below, I have listed some of the international events in which the Alpine competed, but even this is unlikely to be complete as the race organizers have since destroyed their records. The only method of

No one could say that Charles Eyre-Maunsell was not persistent. This time, he failed to finish the 1964 Circuit of Ireland Rally, as just after the photo was taken, he found himself upside down in a ditch. (Charles Eyre-Maunsell)

Charles Eyre-Maunsell puts the Alpine through its paces on one of the hill climbs in the 1965 Circuit of Ireland Rally. (Charles Eyre-Maunsell)

research open to me was to check the entry lists given in magazines of the day. In the case of rallies, the cars were normally listed by the name of Sunbeam only and so it was not always possible to ascertain whether they were Alpines or Rapiers.

Summary of International Events in which Alpines Competed between 1959 and 1963

Car no.	Reg. no.	Event	Dates	Drivers	Placing and awards
15	XWK 418	R.A.C. Rally	17.11.59 to 20.11.59	Ray/Crabtree	5th in class
21				Fraser/Shenley-Price	3rd in class
61		29th Monte Carlo Rally	18.1.60 to 24.1.60	Sunley/Piggott	96th overall
111	W.60148			Backlund/Falk	Class win: Riviera Cup: Moulins Cup: Challenge Automobile Club Van Deutschland E.V. Cup: Challenge de L'Automobile Club de Swisse Cup: Challenge Automobile Club de Portugal Cup.
203				Trigg/Miller	'Securite Routier' award
290				Easton/Whitmore	Crashed
2 further Swedish and 1 Danish Alpines entered, details of which are not known.					
	8363 AZ	International Circuit of Ireland Rally	15.4.60 to 19.4.60	C. W. Eyre Maunsell	3rd in class
				E. T. McMillen	5th in class
		12th International Tulip Rally	2.5.60 to 7.5.60	F. H. Richmond/P. A. Crothall	88th overall
		Greek International Acropolis Rally	May 1960	Nicky Filinis/S. Mourtzopoulis	2nd in class
45	6969 EL	21st International Alpine Rally	27.6.60 to 1.7.60	Mary Handley Page/Pat Ozanne	3rd in class; 3rd in Coupe des Dames; 27th overall classification
21		R.A.C. Rally	21.11.60 to 26.11.60	Rosemary Seers/Pauline Mayman	Believed retired after crash
		30th Monte Carlo Rally	21.1.61 to 24.1.61	Backlund/Falk	Class win and Beach Cup Award
40		Sebring 12-Hour Endurance Race	25.3.61	Leir/Walter	2nd in class
				Hopkirk/Jopp	Retired – cylinder head gasket
41				Wilson/Tamburo	Retired – engine

Car no.	Reg. no.	Event	Dates	Drivers	Placing and awards
42		International Circuit of Ireland Rally	April 1961	Harper/Proctor	3rd in class
				C. N. Eyre-Maunsell/ A. D. Greeves	3rd in class and team award
				E. Dowling	Team award and best performance brake test
		13th Tulip Rally	2.5.61 to 6.5.61	Grimshaw/Beighton	Retired – brakes
		9th Acropolis Rally	18.5.61 to 21.5.61	Filinis/Mourtzopoulos	2nd in class
				Banks/Blaydon	Crashed
4	2 BUS	International Scottish Rally	22.5.61 to 24.5.61	John Melvin/Anne Melvin	Outright win and class win
12	200 MKL			T. A. Crawford	Not known
34	3000 RW	Le Mans 24-Hour Race	10.6.61 to 11.6.61	Harper/Proctor	Winner Index of Thermal Efficiency Cup
35	3001 RW	22nd Alpine Rally	24.6.61 to 28.6.61	Hopkirk/Jopp	Disqualified
				Mary Handley Page/ Pauline Meyman	2nd in Coupe Des Dames
				Jack Brabham/Stirling Moss	3rd in class
		Riverside 3-Hour Grand Prix D'Endurance			Class win
					3rd overall
116		R.A.C. Rally	13.11.61 to 18.11.61	Pollard/	Not known
87	2 BUS	Monte Carlo Rally	21.1.62 to 27.1.62	Grimshaw/Ralphs	3rd in class
175				J. Melvin/G. Bennet	3rd in class
121	526 GMP			G. Grant/C. Davis	5th in class
41		Sebring 12-Hour Endurance Race	March 1962	Rossdale/Freeman	Finished: place unknown
				Peter Harper/Peter Proctor	3rd in class
42				Payne/Sheppard	15th overall
43				Miles/Spencer	32nd overall
44				Theodolio/Barrette	Retired – broken con rod
					33rd overall
		14th Tulip Rally	6.5.62 to 11.5.62	Grimshaw/Ralphs	Retired
		Nurburgring 1000 kms Race	27.5.62	Miller/Shaffer	29th overall
		International Scottish Rally	11.6.62 to 15.6.62	Mr. & Mrs. Melvin	Retired – damaged radiator
		Columbian Canyon Rally	1962		Team prize
		Tuscon Sports Car Race	1962		1st, 2nd, 3rd.

Car no.	Reg. no.	Event	Dates	Drivers	Placing and awards
		Mexico Rally	1962	Paul Romero/Alfonso Romero	Outright win
		Westwood, Vancouver, Modified Production Car Race	1962		Class win
32	9202 RW	Le Mans 24 Hours	23.6.62 to 24.6.62	Harper/Proctor	15th overall
33	9203 RW			Hopkirk/Jopp	Retired – engine
		Tour de France	15.9.62 to 23.9.62	Nail/Francais	Retired – ignition (just prior to final control)
51	9202 RW	R.A.C. Rally	12.11.62 to 17.11.62	Rosemary Smith/ Rosemary Seers	4th overall
48	MEL 63			G. Grant/P. Pilsworth	Retired – split petrol tank
73	1 EGG			J. Melvin/W. Bennett	Not known
		Canadian Grand Prix Production Car Race		Denny Coad	2nd overall Class win
55		32nd Monte Carlo	21.1.63 to 24.1.63	Gregory Grant/Tom Wisdom	Retired – crew fatigue
		Sebring	25.3.63 to 26.3.63	Jerry Titus/Dave Jorden	3rd in class
				Bill Kneeland/Filippo Theodoli	4th in class
		Circuit of Ireland	13.4.63 to 16.4.63	Charles Eyre-Maunsell/ Alex Spence	Retired – back axle
32	9202 RW	Le Mans	15.6.63 to 16.6.63	Tiny Lewis/Keith Balisat	Retired – broken crankshaft
33	9201 RW			Peter Harper/Peter Proctor	Retired – cylinder head gasket
		Scottish Rally	3.6.63 to 7.6.63	Rosemary Smith/Elma Lewsey	Retired – radiator
		Tour de France	17.9.63 to 26.9.63	Rosemary Smith/ Margaret Mackenzie	Winner Coupe des Dames 3rd overall on Monaco Circuit Race 1st overall on scratch 1st overall on handicap

5
Special Tuning

Two stages of engine tuning and associated kits of parts were available for the Series 2 Alpine, for owners who wished to improve road performance or enter their cars in circuit racing events.

Full details of the contents of kits are given in the next few pages. I

Alpines competed in many hundreds (if not thousands) of events with tremendous success. They responded extremely well to tuning — at Le Mans, they achieved over 120 m.p.h. down the Mulsanne straight.

have also included the respective part numbers since although these parts can no longer be ordered from Talbot Ltd., dealers may still have some among their redundant stock. The remainder of the chapter explains how to modify an Alpine using existing parts or suitable alternative parts which are still available from other sources.

Fitting the works kits was not advised by the Rootes Group until the engine had been progressively run in and had completed 4,000 miles. If it was necessary to fit the kits at a lower mileage, the clearances of the pistons and piston rings had first to be checked. For those readers who are contemplating fitting a replacement engine into an Alpine and wish to special tune it before fitting, I have included full details on how to check these clearances.

Tuning Kits (that were available)
Stage I Engine Tuning Kit
Stage II Engine Tuning Kit
Stage II Engine Tuning Kit (U.S.A.)
Oil Cooler Kit
Brake Lining Kit
Rear Axle Kit (disc wheels only)
Suspension Kit

Item	No. per set	Part number
Engine Tuning Kit (Stage I)		
Camshaft	1	1208620
Camshaft thrust plate	1	P103613
Distributor	1	1216047
Champion N3 sparking plug	4	
Air cleaner	2	1208711
Plug – cylinder head	1	9803045
Washer – cylinder head	1	9077039
Plug – water pump	1	9805031
Carburettor parts		
Choke tubes 30 mm (only needed on cars fitted with W1A type carburettors and air cleaner.)	2	
Metering jet (150)	2	
Main discharge tube (3.5 mm OE)	2	
Blanking plug (By-pass)	2	
High speed bleed (70)	2	
Diaphragm gasket	2	
Return spring – rear carb. choke lever	1	

Engine Tuning Kit (Stage II)

Flywheel assembly (not in U.S.A. kit)	1	1208623
Clutch cover assembly	1	1800247
Clutch driven plate	1	1800259
Engine stabilizer comprising the following parts:		
Torque restrictor arm	1	1206317
Torque restrictor rubber	1	P113421
Washer – plain	1	9067037
Shakeproof washer	2	9664242
Nut – restrictor rubber	2	9510060

Engine Oil Cooler Kit

Adaptor plate – cylinder block	1	1206318
Union – adaptor plate	2	9152007
Washer – union	2	9077616
Joint – adaptor plate	2	1207973
Bolt – filter and adaptor plate to cylinder block	4	19105221
Oil cooler ⎫	1	1201367
Bolt ⎪	4	19004045
Washer ⎬ Oil cooler to bracket	4	9067015
Washer ⎪	4	9664162
Nut ⎭	4	9600041
Support bracket – Oil cooler	2	1201368
Bolt ⎫	4	19004045
Washer ⎬ Bracket to panel	4	9664162
Nut ⎭	4	9600041
Hose – filter to cooler	1	1201369
Hose – cooler to engine	1	1201370

Brake Lining Kit

Brake pad	4	5039424

Rear Axle Kit (Disc wheels only – 17 or 25 spline kit)

Axle shaft c/w sleeve	2	
Key	2	9213033
Hub assembly	2	1216507

Important Note

The inner ends of the axle shafts and differential gears used on these cars have either 17 or 25 splines. Separate kits are available to meet these conditions and a check should be made to see which kit is needed.

Axle shaft identification is by a letter stamped on the outer end which is visible after removing the nave plate. The letters used are:

Standard axle shafts – 17 spline B*

25 spline E

Competition axle shafts – 17 spline G   5220527

25 spline P   5220587

(*Shafts without a letter have 17 splines)

Suspension Kit

Front springs	2	1206310
Front anti-roll ($\frac{7}{8}$-in. dia.)	1	1206311
Roll bar rubbers ($\frac{27}{32}$ in. hole)	4	1206301
Shock absorber – rear R.H.	1	1206306
Shock absorber – rear L.H.	1	1206307

Engine Tuning Stages

Stage I: Modify carburettor settings.

Change camshaft and distributor.

Clean up inlet and exhaust parts in the cylinder head.

Fit Champion N3 sparking plugs.

Renew big end bolts and nuts.

Blank off water flow to inlet manifold (only for racing).

Stage II: Fit lightened flywheel.

Fit competition clutch which has stronger springs to increase its 'clamping' load.

Dynamically balance crankshaft, flywheel and clutch assembly.

Fit engine stabilizer.

Note: The oil cooler kit should be fitted after either Stage I or Stage II tuning if continuous use of high r.p.m. is intended.

Fitting Tuning Parts to Engine

The extent to which the engine is dismantled depends upon what parts are being fitted.

Stage I tuning can be carried out with the engine in the car. Stage II tuning requires the removal of the engine. If both stages of tuning are undertaken at the same time, the engine should be removed first.

Engine Performance

After this rather 'mild' factory tuning kit was fitted to the Series 2 Alpine, it gave the following engine power output data:

B.h.p. (gross)   86 @ 5,000 r.p.m.   101 @ 6,000 r.p.m.

B.h.p. (nett)	80 @ 5,000 r.p.m.	94.1 @ 6,000 r.p.m.
B.m.e.p.	146 @ 3,800 r.p.m.	147 @ 4,500 r.p.m.
Max torque (lb./ft.)	94 @ 3,800 r.p.m.	94.9 @ 4,500 r.p.m.

Pistons – Checking Clearance

This check is necessary only when the engine mileage is below 4,000 miles.

Pistons are fitted to new engines with a skirt clearance of .0010 in.–.0018 in. but for engines in which the main requirement is maximum performance, pistons should have a skirt clearance of .0018–.0020 in. In the absence of suitable measuring equipment such as a ring gauge, cylinder bore clock gauge and external micrometer, piston clearance can be checked in the following manner:

1. Pistons should be thoroughly cleaned.
2. Cylinder bores should be wiped dry from oiled condition.
3. Insert piston upside down into the cylinder bore with a strip of $\frac{1}{2}$ in. wide × .0015 in. thickness feeler strip, between the maximum thrust side of the piston and the cylinder bore. The piston should be at the bottom of the bore. A pull of $\frac{1}{2}$lb. to 1$\frac{1}{2}$lb. on a spring balance will be required to pull the feeler out if the clearance is .0018 in–.0020 in.
4. Any pistons found with less clearances than that previously given should be replaced by fitting 'down graded' pistons.
5. If replacement pistons are fitted each piston must be of similar weight.

   The fitting of 'down graded pistons' will probably give some increase in oil consumption.

   Before fitting the new pistons with their new rings, the glaze on the cylinder bores must be removed. This can be done with No. 1 or No. 1$\frac{1}{2}$ grade emery paper wrapped around a dummy wooden piston, moved up and down the bore, and rotated first one way then the other, to give criss-crossed abrasions.

Top Piston Rings

Where it is necessary to remove the pistons for checking their clearances, the top piston ring gaps should be checked. These should not be less than .025 in.

Camshafts

Changing the camshaft to one that gives considerably more engine power output over the medium and high speed range will interfere with low speed power and the engine's flexibility. The cams have no quietening ramps and in consequence the valve gear is not so quiet in operation as the standard camshaft.

Three versions of camshafts were used throughout the production of the Alpine. They had the following valve timings:

	Up to Chassis No. B94100000	*From B94100000 to B39500000*	*From B39500000 to end of production*
Inlet opens	14 b.t.d.c.	19 b.t.d.c.	29 b.t.d.c.
Inlet closes	52 a.b.d.c.	57 a.b.d.c.	63 a.b.d.c.
Exhaust opens	56 b.b.d.c.	61 b.b.d.c.	69 b.b.d.c.
Exhaust closes	10 a.t.d.c.	15 a.t.d.c.	23 a.t.d.c.

The camshaft which was offered in the Series 2 Alpine tuning kit had the following valve timings:

Inlet opens	25 b.t.d.c.
Inlet closes	59 a.b.d.c.
Exhaust opens	63 b.b.d.c.
Exhaust closes	21 a.t.d.c.

Like most parts for the Alpine, these camshafts are no longer available from Talbot Ltd. However, numerous firms throughout the U.K., if not the world, can offer camshafts to the Alpine enthusiast who wishes to tune his Alpine. I talked to three such firms who can offer a world-wide service: Piper Engineering, Eddie Dench of Burtons, and Jeff Howe of Howe Exhausts.

The camshafts these firms offer mainly fall into three categories and have the following valve timings:

	Burtons	*Piper*	*Howe*
'Street' category:			
Inlet opens		37 b.t.d.c.	30 b.t.d.c.
Inlet closes		75 a.b.d.c.	60 a.b.d.c.
Exhaust opens		75 b.b.d.c.	60 b.b.d.c.
Exhaust closes		37 a.t.d.c.	30 a.t.d.c.
Valve lift		.387	.435
'Fast Road/Rally' category:			
Inlet opens	29 b.t.d.c.	32 b.t.d.c.	35 b.t.d.c.
Inlet closes	88 a.b.d.c.	68 a.b.d.c.	65 a.b.d.c.
Exhaust opens	67 b.b.d.c.	68 b.b.d.c.	65 b.b.d.c.
Exhaust closes	50 a.t.d.c.	32 a.t.d.c.	35 a.t.d.c.
Valve lift	.415	.430	.435
'Full Race' category:			
Inlet opens	43 b.t.d.c.	42 b.t.d.c.	40 b.t.d.c.

Inlet closes	84 a.b.d.c.	78 a.b.d.c.	80 a.b.d.c.
Exhaust opens	84 b.b.d.c.	82 b.b.d.c.	80 b.b.d.c.
Exhaust closes	43 a.t.d.c.	38 a.t.d.c.	40 a.t.d.c.
Valve lift	.480	.440	

Whereas the tuning kits had only the one camshaft available in what would now be considered 'mild' specifications, it was very carefully designed and considered the most suitable for both road and competition use at that time. These three firms offer a greater variety of camshafts up to what must be considered 'hairy' specifications, thus allowing the owner to choose according to which stage of tune he requires.

Changing the Camshaft
Remove front grille.
Remove radiator.
Remove crankshaft pulley and timing cover.
Remove timing wheels and chain (note oil thrower in front of crankshaft sprocket).
Remove sump, oil pump and distributor.
Remove camshaft thrust plate.
Remove cylinder head, rocker shaft and pushrods.
Remove tappet cover and cam followers.
Remove fuel pump.
Withdraw camshaft.

The procedure for fitting the new camshaft is the reverse of the above. However, before this is done, each cam and cam follower should be thoroughly smeared with colloidal graphite or a similar substance such as Wynnes engine oil additive, as this will assist in the initial lubrication of these parts when the engine is started.

Also check for wear on the cam follower faces: these should show a highly polished finish. Renew any that show signs of pitting or wear, and also renew the camshaft thrust plate – do not replace the old one.

Before replacing the timing wheels, the hole in the cylinder block, through which the timing chain oil feed pipe passes, should be blanked off. This is to prevent a pressure build-up in the timing case, which can cause oil leakage past the crankshaft pulley oil return scroll. This can be done as shown in fig. 1. The blanking plate is made from 16 SWG mild steel sheet and is held in place by the union. A small slot is cut into the plate to allow insertion of the bent end of the feed pipe.

When replacing the timing wheels and chain, the camshaft sprocket must be pulled onto the camshaft by using a nut, plate and suitable length of threaded rod screwed into the front of the camshaft. If this sprocket is driven on the camshaft, the camshaft will move backwards and remove the large core plate at the rear end of the rear bearing of the camshaft. Fig. 2 shows the timing wheels with the timing marks correctly positioned.

After refitting the timing chain and timing wheels, the camshaft endfloat should be checked with a dial gauge. It should be .002 in–.003 in.

BLANKING PLATE

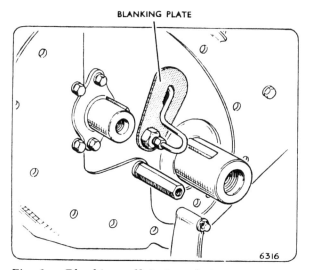

6316

Fig. 1. Blanking off timing chain oil pipe hole.

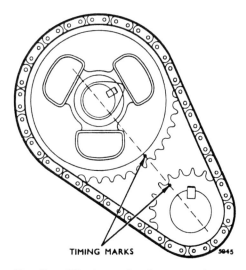

TIMING MARKS

Fig. 2. Timing wheels correctly fitted.

Cylinder Head

Although there are numerous firms on the market which can supply staged cylinder heads for the Alpine, this is the procedure if you wish to do it yourself:

Remove manifolds and carburettors as complete assembly.

Remove valves.

File or grind away any casting roughness in the inlet and exhaust ports in the cylinder head. Also modify these ports by removing any surplus metal found in places A and B as shown in fig. 3.

The valves should be faced up and the valve seats reground and checked for concentricity. Lightly grind in valves and check for seating.

The rating of the standard valve springs is quite satisfactory for competition work, but you should replace your old springs with new ones to obtain peak efficiency.

While the cylinder head is off, a check should be made of the manifold to cylinder head gasket to ensure that it does not protrude over the port holes. A further check should be made to ensure that the inlet and exhaust manifold ports line up to the cylinder head ports, as there must be no steps or edges to impede the incoming mixture or outgoing exhaust gas. This check can be made by locating the manifold gasket on the cylinder head stud holes and checking the cylinder head port hole alignment to the gasket port holes. The manifold gasket is then located on the inlet and exhaust manifold fixing holes and the manifold port holes compared with the port hole positions in the manifold gasket. Any misalignment of the ports will then be apparent and any steps or edges that could oppose gas flow should be carefully filed away.

For racing events, where water heated manifolds are fitted, blank off the water feed to the inlet manifold by fitting blanking plugs in place of the water pump and cylinder head union connections.

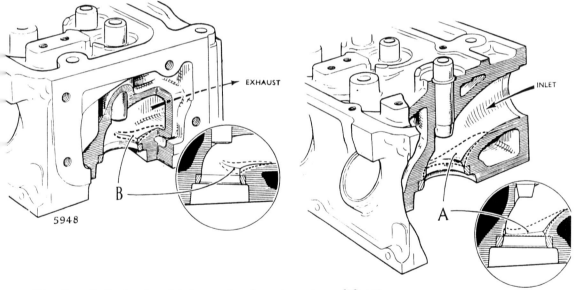

Fig. 3.   Cylinder head inlet and exhaust port modification.

Distributor

Unfortunately, the distributor specified in the works tuning kit can no longer be obtained from Lucas and they cannot recommend any alternative. The replacement unit gives a modified advanced curve which suits the change of camshaft, for those readers who are lucky enough to find these parts locally. The distributor gives the following advance figures while it is decelerating or reducing vacuum.

Distributor r.p.m.	Distributor advance	Inches of mercury	
Run up to 2,250 r.p.m.	13° to 15°	Adjust to 8.25 ins.	4° to 6°
Decelerate to 1,900 r.p.m.	12° to 14°	Reduce to 7.0 ins.	3° to 5°
Decelerate to 800 r.p.m.	9° to 11°	Reduce to 5.0 ins.	$\frac{1}{2}$° to 3°
Decelerate to 500 r.p.m.	$5\frac{1}{2}$° to 9°		
Decelerate to 400 r.p.m.	0° to $3\frac{1}{2}$°		

Carburation

Correct carburation must be considered the essence of an efficient engine, whether it be for road or track use. Choosing which type of carburation to use for your modified Alpine can be a traumatic task as so many conversions were marketed. I have already described how the Series 1, 2 and early Series 3 Alpines were fitted with Zenith carburettors, the late Series 3 and Series 4 Alpines with the twin choke Solex, and lastly the Series 5 with twin Strombergs. With so many changes in types of carburettors, not to mention the variations in jet sizes fitted, it is easy to see that the carburation for the Alpine caused many problems for the Rootes engineers, owing to the limited types they were allowed to use. You have a wider selection, as you will read. With all the conversions, the selection of jet sizes will depend on the degree of tune you select for your car. Where jet sizes are mentioned, these have been considered 'a good starting point' to work from and it is left to you to find the most suitable for your particular vehicle – especially if you are tuning for competition use.

Twin Zenith Carburettors

The Zenith carburettors were undoubtedly a good choice for the early Alpine, especially the Series 2, and when correctly jetted can give both power and economy. This was proved at Le Mans in 1961, but was it the best choice? Many people will say no, while just as many would say yes. Over the next few pages I will try to describe in detail the choice of conversions the Alpine owner had to choose from, those which the engineers did not. All these conversions can still be obtained.

For those who wish to retain the original Zenith carburettor, obtain the items as described under 'Engine tuning kit Stage II' and fit as follows.

Twin Zenith carburettors, as fitted to the Series 1 and 2, and part of the Series 3. This may not be the ultimate carb. set-up, but it certainly performed well at Le Mans.

This conversion is also suitable for all Alpines fitted with Zenith carburettors although the advantages would not be as great on the Series 3 as on the Series 2.

While the manifolds are off, the carburettors should be removed and the carburettor flange faces and inlet manifold faces checked for flatness using a surface plate and marking. The use of a straight edge is not sufficient.

Examine the air intake bore of each carburettor to see that they are free from casting roughness or flashes.

Remove the carburettor throttle bodies and the screws locating the choke tubes. While the throttle bodies are removed, carefully scrape away any tarnish deposited in the throttle bores, taking care not to damage the slow running and progression hole outlets. Screw back the throttle stop screws and ensure that the throttles are properly centralized in their bores. Fit new heat resisting joints between the carburettor bodies and throttle bodies. A thin smear of jointing should be used on these faces and care is needed to prevent the jointing from entering the carburettor passage-ways. Due to the compression of the heat resisting joint, the four cheese-headed screws holding the throttle body to the carburettor body must be tightened by using a spanner on the screwdriver. The use of the screwdriver alone is not sufficient.

Remove items 3, 4 and 5 if fitted, and 7. The high speed bleeds (7) should be pulled out with large pliers, pincers, or side cutting wire cutters, which of course destroys them. Replace all these items with the parts or jets recommended. If the main discharge jets (3) cannot be pushed out after removing the metering jets (4), a taper tread tap may be screwed into its lower end to allow the jets to be pulled out.

When fitting the replacement high speed bleed (7), a suitable recessed punch (8) must be used as shown in fig. 4.

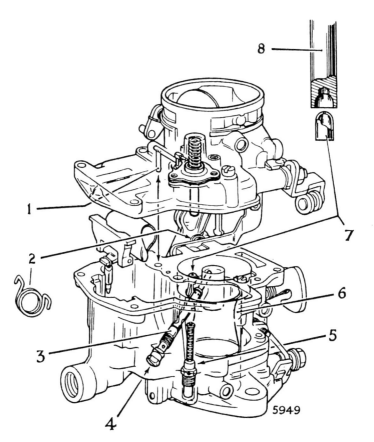

Fig. 4. Ghost view of Zenith W.I.A. type carburettor passageways and jet positions. W.I.P. type carburettors are similar except for item 5 and its operating diaphragm, plunger, spring and spring cover.

The blanking plate and joint or diaphragm must effectively seal off the passage way (1) which is always at inlet manifold vacuum. This is about 16 in. Hg. on idling and even more under closed throttle over run conditions.

Fit the choke control lever spring (2) to the choke control lever on the rear carburettor.

Replace the carburettor top body to the main body joints.

Ensure that the throttle on the front carburettor opens to a gap of .025 in. when the strangler lever is pulled fully over. A no. 72 drill can be used to check the throttle gap between the throttle edge and throttle bore, and any adjustment needed can be made by altering the throttle connecting rod position in the strangler lever. This throttle setting is made to bring the throttles into the correct position for cold starting when the choke is fully out.

Check that the carburettor flange joints fit correctly on the carburettor flange and inlet manifold flange. Check that the bores in the inlet manifold line up to the throttle bores in the carburettor. This is done by holding the throttle fully open and shining a light down the carburettor air intake

Refit the inlet and exhaust manifold to the cylinder head with a new joint.

Adjust both carburettors' slow running speed screws so that each throttle is open .003 in. at the maximum diameter at right angles to the throttle spindle axis.

Replace both carburettors without altering the slow running throttle screw settings. New joints should be fitted at the flange joints between the carburettors and inlet manifold. When tightening the clamp bolts, adjacent to the flexible disc coupling, ensure that the two throttle stop screws are hard against their stops and the throttles are absolutely free to move. Incorrect coupling of the carburettors can cause considerable binding and wear of the throttle spindles.

Adjust the rod connecting the choke levers so that both choke operating cams are against their off position stops together.

Important note After the carburettor tops have been taken off from either carburettor in position, never depress the accelerator pump piston, with the accelerator pump discharge nozzle removed. If the accelerator pump piston is depressed in this condition, the small ball valve may be lifted off its seat and fall into the inlet manifold. From here it can enter a cylinder and ruin a piston. This ball valve is easily lost even while dismantling the carburettors after they have been removed. It has no spring above it.

The Alpine's 1592-c.c. engine and gearbox unit. When fitted with the twin choke Solex compound carburettor, it failed to live up to expectations.

Twin Choke Solex Carburettor
Fitted to the Alpine in attempt to gain better fuel economy, this carburettor never did work out as well as Rootes expected; in fact, it was more of a disaster. Although it did return slightly better fuel consumption figures when new, on the Series 3 as compared to the Series 4, its life span is very low, and it is not suitable for any degree of tune. Thus, I would suggest replacing it with one of the other conversions.

Twin Stromberg C.D. 150 Carburettors
This is quite a lively carburettor, which returned better fuel consumption figures for the larger engined Series 5 Alpine than those of the Series 4. However, it still did not match the figures returned by the Series 2 Alpine, and that includes performance.

Weber 28/36 D.C.D. Carburettor
This was offered by numerous firms as a conversion for the late Series 3 and 4 Alpines fitted with the twin choke Solex carburettor. The advantage of this carburettor, apart from giving a noticeable increase in both fuel economy and performance, is that its base is identical to that of the Solex and therefore allows the carburettors to be interchanged using the existing manifold, thereby cutting down the cost of the conversion.

I spoke to Ted Napper and Stuart Derrington of V.W. Derringtons, the tuning specialists, who still market this conversion and they recommend the following jet sizes for the 28/36 D.C.D.:

Venturi	26 m.m.	27 m.m.
Main jet	140	160
Emulsion tubes	F30	F30
Air correction jet	220	180
Slow running jet	50	70
Pump jet	70	

Twin Weber 40 DCOE Carburettors

This must be considered the ultimate in carburettor conversions marketed for the Alpine and is a must if you are considering using your Alpine in competition. Jack Brabham first marketed this conversion for the Series 2 Alpine. It increased performance tremendously, without much loss of fuel consumption. Road tests show that Brabham's conversion under test conditions returned better fuel consumption than that of the standard Series 3 Alpine. However, like all other complex machinery, the DCOE must be looked after and set up correctly to obtain the best results. V.W. Derringtons still market this conversion and Ted Napper recommends the following jet sizes:

Auxiliary venturi	3.5
Venturi (choke)	30 m.m.
Main jet	120
Emulsion tubes	F16
Air correction jet	175
Slow running jet	45F9
Pump jet	45

Twin 1½″ S.U. Carburettors

Several companies marketed this conversion with some success, although no performance figures are available for the Alpine. Alexander Engineering Ltd., one of these companies, published the following figures for the Sunbeam Rapier 111:

m.p.h.	*Standard*	*Converted*
0–50	11.7 secs.	10.00 secs.
0–60	16.5 secs.	14.1 secs.
0–70	24.9 secs.	19.2 secs.
0–80	39.9 secs.	27.00 secs.

They stated that 'The Alpine's performance figures are improved in the same proportion.'

The conversion consisted of no more than replacing the existing manifold and carburettors. It was first marketed for the Series 2 Alpine and carried on being sold throughout the Alpine range, although on the introduction of the Series 5 it was reduced to 'the $1\frac{1}{4}$' S.U.s, for economy rather than power. I consider the S.U. carburettor to be very responsive. It reacts very well to tuning, and is easy to maintain, and although not as powerful as the twin Webers, it is well worth considering. As far as I can ascertain, only Howe Exhaust market the inlet manifold for this conversion, though of course the S.U.s are available everywhere. Selecting the needle size and spring will, I'm afraid, have to be a matter of trial and error as no details are available.

Flywheel
The flywheel should be lightened by machining it to the dimensions shown in fig. 5, after which it should be balanced statically and

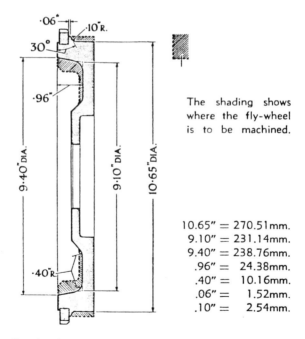

The shading shows where the fly-wheel is to be machined.

10.65" = 270.51mm.
9.10" = 231.14mm.
9.40" = 238.76mm.
.96" = 24.38mm.
.40" = 10.16mm.
.06" = 1.52mm.
.10" = 2.54mm.

Fig. 5. *The flywheel should be machined to the above dimensions to lighten it.*

dynamically. The following procedure should then be carried out:

1. Bolt the flywheel on to the crankshaft and check the flywheel run out with a clock gauge. This must not exceed .003 in. when measured at the outer diameter of the clutch lining face.
2. The four flywheel fixing bolts must be tightened to 40 lb/ft. torque.
3. After bolting on the replacement clutch pressure plate assembly to the flywheel, the crankshaft, flywheel, and the clutch pressure plate should be checked for dynamic balance as a complete assembly.

Clutch and Brake Units
The works stage two kit contained a clutch pressure plate fitted with stronger springs to ensure freedom from clutch slip. It also contained a special competition type driven plate, and harder type brake pads, although needless to say these can no longer be obtained through dealers. I discussed this point with John Holroyd, the specialist from Automotive Products Racing Division. Although he could not recommend a suitable alternative at the time of asking, John could not have been more helpful. He is only too willing to assist any Alpine owner wishing to find a clutch unit/brake pads suitable for competition use. Unlike most parts manufacturers, A.P. Racing recognize the need of classic car owners. If they no longer market the parts you require, they will show you what is needed to modify your existing flywheel and if necessary clutch controls, to allow you to fit parts which are still available.

Re-assembling Engine
Replace the crankshaft. Tighten the main bearing bolts to 50/60 lb./ft. and check the crankshaft endfloat which should be .002 in–.004 in. The higher limit is preferable for high performance running.

Replace the pistons and connecting rods. It is very easy to break the thin edges of the oil scraper rings if an improvised ring compressor is used. Extreme care should therefore be taken when replacing piston rings.

Fit new big end bolts and nuts. Tighten these nuts to a torque loading of 25 lb./ft. The threads must be perfectly clean and lightly oiled before the nuts are tightened.

Replace the oil pump. To ensure correct engagement of the oil pump drive gear with its driving gear on the camshaft, the engine should be turned to the no. 1 firing t.d.c. position and the oil pump gear positioned so that its distributor driving slots are as shown in fig. 6 when the pump is bolted on.

Replace the sump.

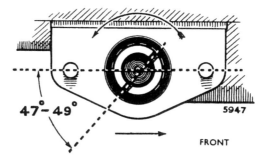

Fig. 6.   *Oil pump driving slots at No. 1 firing position t.d.c., as seen after removing distributor.*

Replace the distributor and fuel pump.

Replace the oil thrower on the crankshaft and timing cover. The cover must be centralized to the crankshaft with the Churchill tool, R.G. 89.

Replace the cylinder head, tightening the fixing bolts to a torque of 45 lb./ft. The cyclinder head bolts must always be tightened while the engine is cold and the tightening sequence repeated until you are sure that each bolt carries the correct torque loading.

Replace the engine.

Engine Stabilizer

Fit the engine stabilizer to the cylinder head as shown in fig 7 using the bracket as a template to determine where the $\frac{3}{8}$ in. dia. hole in the bulkhead should be drilled. This will require the fitting of another long stud at the forward fixing point. The bracket must be bolted on top of the two cylinder head nuts with two extra washers and nuts, and NOT directly onto the cylinder head. It may be necessary to move the choke operating cable slightly to the nearside.

Fig. 7.   *Engine stabilizer in position.*

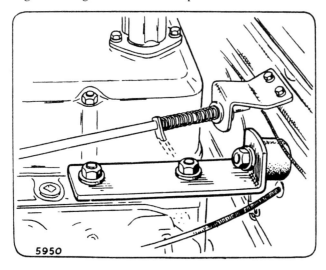

Rear Axle

This section applies only to those vehicles fitted with disc wheels. The replacement axle shafts which were supplied in this kit had their 'zone' of hardening extended to increase their strength still further. The replacement hubs and driving keys were also hardened. (Wire wheels are automatically treated in this way.)

Again, these cannot be bought off the shelf, but it is advisable to have these parts hardened if very high cornering forces will be encountered, as in circuit racing. Most large engineering firms will advise on this. If you have any difficulty, contact Alan Pickford of Pickford Axle Exchange.

Since a great deal of information is required to remove, dismantle, rebuild and refit the rear axle, you are advised to refer to the official workshop manual.

Oil Cooler

Where the engine is required to run at almost continuous high r.p.m., such as in circuit racing or on long mountain climbs, an oil cooler kit must be fitted.

The oil cooler should be mounted in front of the radiator so that it is in the air stream passing through the front grill. It is connected by flexible piping to a special adaptor block fitted between the filter base and cylinder block.

All oil delivered by the oil pump is passed through the oil filter and then passed to the oil cooler and the oil gallery in the engine. This ensures that the oil feed to all the bearings will be cooled. The manufacturers state that the actual temperature reduction of the oil is approximately 35° F.

Fig. 8. Oil cooler fitted in position, oil cooler pipe connections and pipe run.

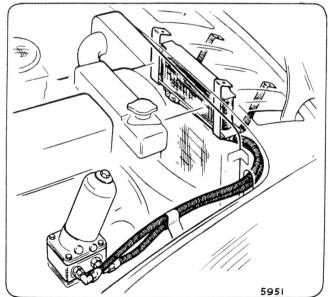

5951

Suspension

As the Alpine you own or will be buying will be between 12 and 21 years' old, the suspension may require attention. The dampers may be worn out and the springs weak. If you are intending to use the car in any type of competition, you should obtain up-rated replacement springs. If you cannot buy the front springs locally, they can be obtained from Quality Carsprings. This company has assured me that all the springs they supply are made to suit individual customers' requirements; if you send them one of your old springs with full details of the car (make, model, c.c., weight) and details of what use you are going to put the car to, they will uprate the springs specially for that purpose. New rear springs need not be uprated as the original design is quite adequate. Replacements for these can be obtained from Britannia Spring Engineering Co.

Shock absorbers should be replaced with adjustable types such as Spax or Koni. This will enable you to find the most suitable stiffness setting to suit your requirements.

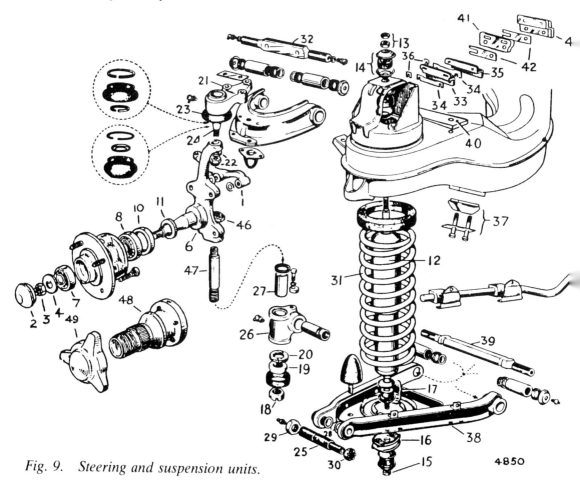

Fig. 9.   Steering and suspension units.

Front Shock Absorber Removal
1. Load the vehicle to a laden condition.
2. Undo the two nuts (13) at the upper spindle fixing and remove the upper rubber and cup washers (14). Slacken the two nuts at the lower spindle fixings (15) (but do not remove).
3. Remove the nuts around the shock absorber lower plate (16). Lift the lower plate to clear the studs and revolve it through 90°, when, due to its shape, it will pass downwards complete with shock absorber and its remaining upper rubber and cup washers (17), through the lower link spring pan.
   Refitting is the reverse of the removal sequence.

To Remove Front Road Springs
1. Remove front shock absorbers.
2. Jack up the car under the front cross member (using a block of wood between the jack and the cross member). Place the car on stands below the side member, and remove road wheels.
3. Fit the spring compressor tool and compress the road springs (31) sufficiently to take the load off the spring.
4. Remove lower link eyebolt (25).
5. Disconnect stabilizer bar and remove four bolts securing bottom link fulcrum pin to the cross member.
6. Release spring compressor gradually until road spring and bottom link can be removed.

To Refit Front Road Springs
Refitting the road springs (31) is a reversal of the above except for the following:
1. Ensure that the rubber insulating ring is in place when positioning the road spring.
2. Compress the spring until the fulcrum pin can be rebolted to the cross member. The bolts should be tightened to 32 lb./ft. and secured with new lock washers.
3. Ensure that sealing rings (28) are correctly fitted when replacing the eyebolt.

Rear Spring Removal and Refitting
Jack up the car and support it by means of chassis stands placed under the chassis frame just forward of the front eyes of the springs.
   Remove road wheels.
   Remove shock absorbers.
   Remove nyloc securing nuts and washers from 'U' bolts.

Jack up rear axle until it is parted from the springs and support it with axle stands.

Remove 'U' bolts.

Tap out lower shackle pins and shakeproof washers after removing nuts with washers, and lower rear end of spring to floor.

Remove front pivot pin in same manner.

Refitting is a direct reversal of the removal operation, but the final tightening of the spring 'U' bolts, shackle assemblies and pivot pins should be carried out after the removal of the jacks and stands, the car standing unladen on the road wheels.

Torque loading for 'U' bolts: 42 lb./ft.

General Recommendations

In addition to the work previously described the following items should be carefully checked and/or considered.

1. Front hub endfloat – this must be checked with a clock gauge. The correct endfloat is .002 in–.003 in.
2. Rear hub nuts should be tightened to a torque of 160/180 lb./ft.
3. Propeller shaft – check the condition of the propeller shaft universal joints and the tightness of the rear universal joint bolts and nuts.
4. Tyres – fit appropriate racing tyres and inflate them to the manufacturer's recommended pressure. In most cases road tyres are not suitable and cannot stand up to track work.
5. Wheel balance – after fitting tyres, wheels should be carefully balanced, both statically and dynamically.
6. Engine r.p.m. – this must not be allowed to exceed 6,000 r.p.m.

The five-bearing crankshaft of the Series 5 certainly made the engine a lot smoother, but there is some debate as to whether it can stand up to the same degree of tune as the three-bearing unit.

7. Weight reduction – in addition to the removal of all loose trim items such as carpets and door trim pads, it is suggested that the heater should be removed. Lighter seats can be fitted if available, and Perspex can be used to replace the door glasses.
   Note: It is not permissible to lighten any part of the engine by drilling.
8. Cylinder head – it is most important that this is pulled down correctly, while the engine is cold, to the torque figure which is recommended by the manufacturer. When this is done, the tightening sequence must be followed several times to ensure that each bolt is correctly tightened and remains so after tightening all other bolts. The cylinder head bolts should be rechecked and reset after the engine has been run in and allowed to become cold.
9. Throttle shaft bracket (Alpines fitted with Zenith carbs.) – this bracket, which is mounted on the front carburettor, should be stiffened up by welding on similar thickness of mild steel as illustrated by the grey parts in fig. 10.
10. Throttle linkage (Zenith carbs.) – a thorough examination should be made of all ball joints and linkage connections to ensure that these items are not worn or assembled incorrectly so as to impair their reliability. Throttle shafts with a ball end are held in the throttle shaft bearing by a 1/16 in. split pin. This pin must be removed and the hole drilled out to take a 3/32 in. split pin. No. 41 drill must be used as the split pin must be a good fit in the hole.

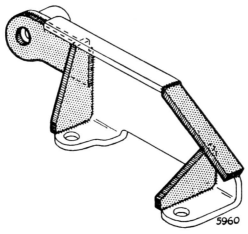

Fig. 10. Throttle shaft bracket on front carburettor — stiffening details.

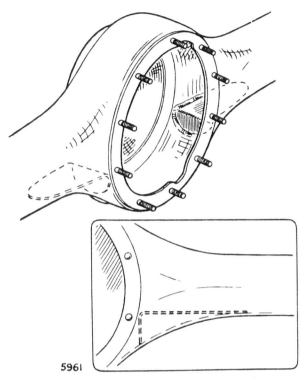

Fig. 11.   Oil baffles welded in position in rear axle housing.

11. Rear axle casing modification – when cornering at very high speeds, i.e. during circuit racing, the centrifugal force is high enough to force the axle oil into the rear banjo tube. This considerably reduces the amount of oil that is lubricating the crown wheel and pinion, and tends to flood the oil seal. To overcome this difficulty, the rear axle should be removed as a complete assembly and once completely dismantled the axle casing should be modified as in fig. 11. This illustration, which is self explanatory, shows how two baffles are welded inside the banjo housing. These baffles prevent the oil from being thrown up into the banjo tubes. They should be made from 12 S.W.G. sheet steel and welded into position. This modification is only needed for high-speed circuit racing.

A great bunch of gentlemen, all specialists in their field, helped me to compile this section of the book. My greatest appreciation goes to:

Ted Napper and Stuart Derrington,
V.W. Derrington Ltd,
63, Alfred Road,
Kingston, Surrey.
Telephone: 01-546 5621/2.

Derringtons are official Weber distributors and can also supply most tuning equipment, including the Piper camshafts and adjustable shock absorbers.

Eddie Dench and Mr. Burton,
Burton Engineering Ltd,
621/631, Eastern Avenue,
Barkingside, Ilford.
Telephone: 01-554 2281/2.

Burtons offer a full tuning facility from crankshaft grinding to building complete performance engines to suit most forms of competition use, as well as supplying the Burton camshafts mentioned.

Jeff Howe,
Jeff Howe Exhausts and Cams Ltd,
Rear Hollyville Cafe
Main Road A20,
West Kingsdown, Kent.
Telephone: West Kingsdown 2347.

Suppliers of one-piece extractor exhaust manifolds, complete exhaust systems, inlet manifolds including those for S.U. carburettors, Howe camshafts and fully worked cylinder heads (customer's own).

John Holroyd,
Automotive Racing Division,
Automotive Products Ltd,
Tachbrook Road,
Leamington Spa,
Warwickshire.

Competition clutch units and brake pads.

Mr. Willis,
Quality Springs Ltd,
St. Georges Road,
Redditch,
Worcestershire B98 8EF.

Front coil springs.

Mr. Jenner,
Britannia Spring & Engineering Co,
Riverside Works,
London Road,
Reading, Berkshire.

Rear leaf springs.

Alan Pickford,
Pickford Axle Exchange,
459 Leyton High Road,
London E18.
Uprated back axles.

To round off the subject of special tuning, I have included the technical history log of one of the Rootes (Canada) works team cars. Driven by Dennis Coad, Craig Fisher and Ian Hart, this car – a Series 2 – had tremendous success throughout the Canadian circuits, competing over the years in many dozens of events (if not hundreds) up until as late as 1975. An interesting point about the car is that its rear wings were modified when the body changes were incorporated in the Series 4 Alpine. Brian Scott of Mississauga, Ontario, Canada was fortunate enough to buy this car, and is now restoring it to its former glory. The log makes interesting reading and we thought we would let you see how the professionals did it:

Section A

Motor Alpine 1600 c.c.
1. Cylinder block bored to 3.2195 ins. equal of 1600 c.c. .035 in. machined from top face of cylinder block to eliminate piston deck height.
2. Top face of cylinder block reworked to prevent masking of exhaust valves.
3. Oil gallery to centre main increased in diameter to 7/16 in.
4. Blanking plate installed at timing chain feed.
5. Crankshaft centre main journal reworked to accept increased oil flow i.e. grove machined in same.
6. Con rods lightened and polished to 1 lb. $7\frac{1}{2}$ oz.
7. Flywheel lightened to 14 lb.
8. Crankshaft lightened, polished and balanced c/w flywheel, clutch assembly, front pulley, rods and pistons.
9. Cylinder head carefully ported to suit Weber manifold.
10. Complete enlarging of inlet and exports carried out.
11. Combustion chambers carefully reworked to prevent masking of inlet valves. Great care then taken in final reworking of chambers to give cubic capacity of 29 c.c.
12. Total of 110 thou. machined from cylinder head to finally arrive at above figure.

Note: Thickness of compressed cylinder head gasket .030 in. = 4 c.c.; compression ratio = 12.12 i.e. 400 ÷ 33.

13. Racing type flat top pistons fitted at a clearance of .003 in − .0035 in.
14. Rootes stage 1 camshaft used with the following specifications: 25 – 59 – 63 – 21 with a valve clearance of 0.41 in.
15. Series 3 Alpine exhaust valves fitted after polishing.
    Note: These valves are .040 in. larger in diameter than standard; they also have chrome stems.
16. Rootes competition oil cooler installed.
17. Fan blades removed.
18. Motor's components carefully cleaned and assembled giving careful attention to all torque values of nuts and bolts.
19. Oil pan deepened and cooling pipes inserted through entire length to assist in oil cooling. Air duct fitted to front grille section to force feed air stream to oil cooler.
20. Oil used in motor B.P. 50 racing oil with S.T.P. added.
21. Special valve springs and caps fitted.
22. Rocker gear lightened and polished.
23. Camshaft followers drilled and lightened.

Motor Alpine 1725 c.c. (fitted in 1966)

Bore = 3.365 ins. (fitted with Volvo 85 m.m. pistons)
Stroke = 3.25 ins.
Cubic capacity = 1892.7 c.c.

Deck height remaining at start of season	= .065 in.
Cubic capacity of combustion chambers	= 33 c.c.
Cubic capacity of head gasket	= 3 c.c.
Cubic capacity of deck height	= 8.183 c.c.
Total upswept volume	44.183 c.c.

Compression ratio = 10.75 : 1

1. Cylinder block machined to accept full crank thrust.
2. Cylinder block machined to unmask exhast valve.
3. 1725 c.c. exhaust valves and inlet valves fitted.
4. Complete motor assembly (moving parts) pro-lube treated.

Section B

Clutch, Transmission and Overdrive

1. Rootes competition close ratio gear set fitted.
2. Rapier II oil splash guard installed.

3. Overdrive rear fixing studs increased in diameter to $\frac{3}{8}$ in. to rear.
4. Reverse lock out installed.
5. Local purchased heavy duty clutch installed, 6 spring type 250 lb. rating.
6. Gear shift top cover extended $3\frac{1}{2}$ ins. to rear.
7. S.A.E. 40 oil used.

Section C

Rear Axle Assembly

1. Diff. ratio of 4.8 : 1 preferred (alternative of 4.44 : 1 used at Mosport)
2. Reworked limited slip diff. assembly fitted (purchased from Rootes, Los Angeles).
3. Axle casing reworked to prevent oil wash to rear hub seals.
4. Radius rod made up and installed from axle casing to frame to prevent axle bounce on acceleration.
5. Rear axle lowered $2\frac{1}{2}$ ins.
6. Diff. oil type S.P. 50136 used with Molyslip added.

Section D

Suspension

1. Rootes competition front coil springs fitted.
2. Rootes heavy duty front sway bar fitted.
3. Gabriel adjustable shock absorbers fitted to front, adjusted to hard position.
4. Rootes competition rear shock absorbers fitted.
5. Front wheel camber adjusted $2\frac{1}{2}°-3°$ neg. toe. in 3/16 in.
6. Remainder of geometry factory specs.
7. Steering column shortened by $4\frac{1}{4}$ ins.

Section E

Tyres and Wheels

1. Dunlop 5.00 $\times$ 13 racing R.S. 6 tyres fitted.
2. Wheel studs replaced by 'Keystone' 7/16 in. $\times$ 20 thread type bolts fitted (Alpine type nuts too short).
3. D.66 type pads fitted.

Section F

Fuel System and Carbs.

1. Twin Weber type D.C.O.E. 42 fitted – basic jets used = main 125 – air bleed 180. These sizes changed according to tune and conditions.
2. S.U. H.D. pusher type fuel pump fitted to rear compartment.
3. Petrol tank filler – altered to centre filling type.
4. Air ram ducting made and fitted to give ram effect and cool air entry to carbs.
   Note: Returned to pair Strombergs for the 1725 c.c. engine as per regs. for production racing.

Section G

Ignition System and Electrical

1. Ignition system converted to transistor type, made by Videolizer Manufacturing Company. Consists of 2×20 amp. transistors, secondary output of coils = 40,000 volts.
2. Set ignition timing to $2°–4°$ in advance of specs.
3. Champion N.3 plugs used with gaps of .040 in.
4. Ignition timing = $16°$ before t.d.c.
5. Lucas B.H.N.O.9A type battery fitted.
6. M.G.A. tachometer fitted 0–7500 r.p.m. re-calibrated to suit Alpine (later replaced by Smiths 0–8000 r.p.m. tell-tale type).
7. All wiring harnesses removed.
8. All non-essential electrical components removed.
9. All remaining components wired separately.
10. Generator mounted but not fitted only acting as jockey pulley.
11. Oil temperature gauge fitted, temp. bulb at oil filter.

Section H

Body Trim

1. Screen removed and racing type made and fitted.
2. All interior upholstery removed.
3. Hood strengthening ribs cut out – hood modified re closing.
4. Trunk lid supports cut out – trunk lock mechanism removed and quick lock catches fitted.
5. Excess Trunk flooring cut out.
6. Excess interior door supports cut out.
7. Roll bar made and installed to C.A.S.C. specs.
8. Aluminium bucket type seat made and fitted.

9. Panelling made and fitted behind driver's seat to rear deck (aluminium used).
10. Grab rail fitted to R.S. of floor.
11. Fire extinguisher fitted to R.S. of floor.
12. L.S. and centre racing type mirrors fitted.
13. Screen mesh fitted to front air ducts.
14. Front and rear bumpers removed.
15. Headlamp assemblies removed and blanking plates fitted.
16. Heater unit c/w controls removed.
17. Screen wipers and mechanism removed.
18. One horn removed.
19. Air ducts made for front disc brakes.

6
What to Look for when Buying an Alpine

Shopping around for an Alpine can be an arduous task, mainly because they are so few and far between; or so it seems from the number of telephone calls I receive from people wishing to buy an Alpine. Although the club likes to hear of Alpines which are being sold, this is mainly to obtain the chassis and registration numbers for our register, which enables us to keep track of the vehicle in the future. So please, no telephone calls, ladies and gentlemen: you must do the searching yourself.

Once you have decided which series Alpine you want to buy, just what do you look for to get value for your money? Even though the Alpine was built to last and built to a superior standard compared to many other marques, like all vehicles made from steel, it is subject to body corrosion and, alas, a lot of Alpines have succumbed to the dreaded attack. So, when shopping around, you should take great care. I will try in this chapter to describe what pitfalls to look for when buying an Alpine, most of which I and my club members have come up against time and time again. If you manage to find an Alpine with all the pitfalls described, you will be looking at one large heap of scrap.

The Chassis
The Alpine's chassis consists of two chassis members running from front to rear of the offside and nearside of the vehicle, plus a very big

The Alpines were solidly built to a very high standard, but now that they are between 12 and 21 years' old, many have succumbed to the dreaded rust bug, and repairs can be expensive. The illustration depicts a ghost view of a Series 3.

cruciform member under the floorpan. Start by checking this cruciform member first. If it is badly corroded, do not buy the car, as this is normally the last to rust, due to the sheer thickness of the metal used.

The two longitudinal members have several corrosion prone spots. First, check the jacking points, both front and rear. As part of the chassis members, these will have been subject to a great deal of stress over the years. A crude but very effective way to check them is obviously to jack up the car, using the official jack. Take each corner in turn and jack it up to the highest point possible. If the chassis is in any way weak and in need of repair, it will creak, if not crumble. It is advisable to get the owner's permission first, as I have seen some disastrous results from this test. If for some reason the owner refuses, don't buy: he has something to hide. Next, follow the chassis members along to the rear spring hangers, and the hanger located closest to the front of the car. This point is also corrosion prone, although it is easier to repair than the jacking points.

Bodywork

Before I go into details of where to look for corrosion in the bodywork, please bear in mind that NO body panels to speak of are available for the Alpine and so all repairs are likely to be expensive.

The front valance takes a great deal of punishment from road dirt and should be looked at thoroughly in its entirety, especially where the panel is welded to the front wings just under the side lights.

The front wings should be examined with great care as these will be the most expensive to repair. Replacement panels would have to be specially made, if you could find a firm to make them, but because of their complex shape very few firms in the U.K. would even try. Check for the tell-tale bubbles around the headlights. If these can be caught early enough, it may be possible to have them leaded in, but if you see any sign of filling by any other method do not buy the car unless you are willing to pay out several hundred pounds. There are two other known but less common points to look for on the front wings: along the top edge of the wing where it folds into a box section for the bonnet to fall into, and down the rear of the wing where the identification badges are located. However, as both these areas are almost flat, unlike the headlamp surrounds, the old metal could be cut out and replaced by new, without many problems.

Lift the bonnet and check the inner wings, the panels between the front wings and the wheel arches. These are the thinnest panels on the car and accordingly rust very badly. They are never a serious problem, as they can be plated without difficulty.

Looking underneath the front wheel arches to the rear of the front wheels, you will see the panels which make up the footwells inside the car. These panels were never welded to the wings but sealed with caulk which becomes brittle over the years and eventually falls away. This can mean rather wet feet on rainy days, but is not a serious problem if caught in time. Check the panels from top to bottom along the edge which rests against the front wings and then lift the front carpets inside the car and check the floorpan at the back of the control pedals.

Door sills, as in all cars, rust in time, but again, this is not a serious problem.

Next, open the doors and take a look at their inner edges. The most vulnerable point is the bottom edge which corrodes when the drainage holes have become blocked, allowing water to build up inside the door itself. The first part to corrode will be the outer skin: look for bubbles on the outer surface of the door. Although a good body shop can make up a new skin, any long-term corrosion will have infected the main door frame as well, making it impossible to remove the outer skin without causing irreparable damage to the frame.

The rear wings have two main corrosion points, the first, as on all vehicles, being the wheel arches. However, corrosion here is not as common as on the lower part of the rear wing, extending from just behind the rear wheel to where it joins the rear valance under the bumper. There are two reasons for this corrosion: the position of the panel means that it takes a great deal of road grime from the rear wheels, while a build-up of water can occur inside the panel itself, probably due to ill fitting or to perished weatherstrips around the boot. Under these conditions, the panel does not have much chance of escape from the attacking rust bug. The rear valance, the panel under the rear bumper, can also be affected in the same way, so it is worth checking it over. Repairable? Well, I have managed to do it. As there are no awkward curves to deal with, it is possible to have sections made up without vast expense.

If you have gone to look at a bad car, you will probably be left with a crumbled heap of scrap metal by the time you reach the next stage, which is the inside of the vehicle. There is not a great deal to look for here, as we have already covered the footwells. Check the seat belt anchorage points on the rear wheel arch by giving them a good hard pull. If they are suspect, the chances are that they will give or, worse still, come away in your hand. This is not a difficult problem to rectify, but worth checking if you think anything of yourself or your passenger. Another point to check is the sealing rubber between the windscreen frame and the scuttle panel to which it is attached. If it is allowing water in, you will see white marks left on the dashboard crash pad. Again, this is not a serious problem to deal with, but to have water drip on your feet every time it rains can be annoying.

3000 RW, the Thermal Efficiency Award winning car, as found on 31st March 1977 by Clive Harrington, the son of its maker. Thinking that this was not a very fitting end for such a famous car, Clive bought it and it is now in the process of being restored. (Clive Harrington).

Straw everywhere, but otherwise complete (the carbs. are in the car). The engine of 3000 RW still had the Le Mans seals intact — an incredible find. (Clive Harrington)

If you are inspecting a Series 3, 4, or 5 Alpine with a hard top, take a look at the rear just behind the quarterlights. This area is always suspect and if the rust bug has been allowed to develop it will allow a substantial amount of water into the car when it rains, and can be very awkward to repair. Although fibreglass hard tops are available at a ridiculously high price, they look dreadful when fitted.

The only other point to look for while inspecting the interior, although nothing to do with bodywork or corrosion, is the window winding mechanism. These tend to fail regularly and replacements are not available.

The Engine

As already described, the Alpine underwent two major engine changes, from the initial 3-bearing 1494 c.c. to the 1592 c.c. of the Series 2, 3 and 4, and finally to the 5-bearing 1725 c.c. of the Series 5.

The engines themselves are incredibly rugged and reliable, having been built for strength and long life rather than very high top speeds (although this can be achieved with the aid of a few refinements as described in Chapter 5).

Every owner will agree that the main problem with any Rootes engine is its tendency to suffer rather badly from oil leaks. The fault lies in the engine design which incorporates a removable valve pushrod inspection cover, even though there is little to inspect and to remove it can be more awkward than removing the entire engine. It is this cover which is responsible for the majority of oil leaks. A great many people ask me where the oil which fills the sparking plug recesses in the cylinder head comes from, and the answer is – this same cover. The bolts holding the cover vibrate loose when the engine is running, allowing oil to escape, and the pressure of the air going through the engine compartment forces the oil up the engine and into the recesses. Once in there, it has no way of escape. The leaks can be stopped quite easily, as follows: remove the cover, obtain a new gasket, clean the area thoroughly, place Hermitite or a similar sealant on both sides of the gasket, replace the cover and new gasket, and using Loctite on the bolts screw them down tightly (not too tightly or they may snap). If this procedure is followed correctly, it will eliminate the leaks for some time, although bolts should be checked regularly. The second likely leaking area is the front timing wheel cover: again, the fault arises when the bolts vibrate loose.

To check wear on the engine internals, start the engine and with the engine idling at working temperature depress the clutch. If the engine revs drop noticeably or, indeed, if the engine stalls, the crank thrust bearing may be worn. More times than not, this would mean that the engine is in need of reconditioning. There are other tests you could make, such as compression tests to check valve seating and cylinder bore condition, but I will not go into details here. It is self-evident that wear occurs in all engines, and reconditioned units are readily available at very reasonable prices.

Steering, Suspension and Brakes
As with all moving mechanical parts, wear in these components is inevitable, although the Alpine does tend to outlive most other marques in this respect. They were, after all, designed for the heavier saloon bodies of the Rapier and Minx. A routine check of the suspension wishbone bushes and fulcrum pins is advisable, as at the time of writing this book these spares are not available in the U.K. Any other faults you may find should be easily repaired if necessary.

Road Test for Checking Gearbox and Back Axle
All gearboxes and back axles used on the Alpine are good, rugged and last well. It is best to check these under road test conditions. The gear changes should be smooth and precise, even when old. Test the overdrive (if fitted) which operates on third and fourth gears: these units are very

reliable providing they have been serviced regularly. The actuating solenoid of the overdrive unit suffers from road filth after a time and should be cleaned and greased regularly, as it could otherwise stop the overdrive from engaging.

Listen out for any whining from the gearbox or the back axle. This could mean that they should be replaced, but there are no problems here apart from the cost.

7
Clubs and Spares

Name of Club	**SUNBEAM ALPINE OWNERS CLUB**
Membership secretary	**Chris McGovern**
Address	**76, Pennine Way, Harlington, Middlesex**
Number of members	**800 plus**
Number of Alpines on register	**1,300 plus (U.K. only)**
Vehicles eligible	**Alpines and Sunbeam Venezias**

Unlike a lot of S.A.O.C. members, I started my Alpining rather late in the Alpine's life. In early 1976 my pride and joy was a Ford Corsair 2000E. One day, when travelling home from work, I was negotiating what was then one of London's busiest roundabouts, Staples Corner, when all of a sudden a Cortina pulled out from the nearside straight into my path. I hit the anchors, came to a standstill, and for a second breathed a sigh of relief. Unfortunately, the driver of a car on my offside was not so quick to respond: he hit the Cortina's offside front and sent it spinning straight back into my offside. My pride and joy was a mess. It transpired the Cortina driver had just passed his driving test and that this was his first experience of driving by himself. When I finally got home, knowing how difficult it is to get money out of insurance companies, I thought I had better find another means of transport. Looking through the classifieds, I decided on the cheapest car advertised, which turned out to be a 1965 Series 4 Sunbeam Alpine, going for £150. After a bit of haggling I got the price down to £125 and I now owned my first Alpine. I must admit it wasn't the car of my dreams but then again you cannot buy a Jensen or an Aston for £125. Actually, it's quite amazing how Alpines do grow on you. What started out as just a means of transport while waiting for the insurance company to pay out was beginning to get more attention than any other car I had owned. All that cleaning and polishing certainly gave it a new lease of life. It took some nine months for the insurance company to pay out on the Corsair, and by then I had become hooked on the Alpine. I promptly sold the Corsair for scrap, and spent the insurance money on renovating the Alpine.

I began to look around for an Alpine Club but without success, for it appeared that everyone was under the impression there was no call for one. Everyone, that is, except *Hot Car* magazine, who suggested I should try to form one. They told me how to go about it, and gave me encouragement by giving me some free publicity in their magazine.

The response was better than I had expected. I received about twenty letters from interested parties and so arranged the first S.A.O.C. meeting. By March, membership was up to about 50. Now only three years later, we are over 800 strong and still growing. I believe I am correct in assuming we are now the biggest one-marque Rootes Club in the world, and we must stand pretty high up in the general classification of all one-marque clubs.

A Sunbeam Venezia, the only other car eligible for S.A.O.C. membership apart from the Alpine, shown here with its owners Keith and Brenda Pountain (just left of centre). This remarkable car has covered less than 2,000 miles since it was made.

Cars belonging to S.A.O.C. members waiting to be judged at the 1978 Thoroughbred and Classic Cars *National Concours, held at Weston Park.*

The biggest obstacle I came up against when starting the club was that of building up a good relationship with Chrysler (U.K.) Ltd. It was like trying to walk through a brick wall – a lot of movement but getting nowhere fast. In addition, bearing in mind the fact that they had disbanded the very active Sunbeam Owner Club after the Rootes takeover, I am sorry to say that the only response I got from our American colleagues was a letter from their legal department, threatening court action if I used the words Sunbeam or Alpine in the club's title. I respond quite well to this type of letter. A lot of correspondence was exchanged over the following months and a mutual agreement over copyright was agreed by September 1977.

The starting of the club was almost certainly a turning point in the Alpine's life, and within a short space of time, with the aid of the publicity the club was getting, the Alpine entered the list of sought-after cars and was soon to be considered a collector's piece. My £125 had turned out to be an investment.

The club's first major outing was when we sent a team to the 1977 *Thoroughbred and Classic Car* event, then held at Weston Park. This was then the largest concours event in the U.K. and numerous predominant members of the motoring world told me that the Alpines did not stand a chance and that I was wrong to enter them, claiming that the competition was too high for us even to be listed. They could not have been more wrong. Mike Green's Series 4 automatic took third place and he followed this up with a fifth place in 1978 and another third in 1979.

Less than a third of the S.A.O.C. members' cars at our 1979 national meeting at Mallory Park circuit. The only let-down was the weather — it rained, and rained, and rained.

Our own first national meeting was held in May 1978 at Donington Park. By this time the club was thriving and had around 250 members (devoted members at that). Despite the fact that these members were scattered throughout the British Isles, we still managed to turn out almost 100 Alpines and about 300 people. The meeting was a tremendous success. It all started on a Saturday morning, with a concours judged by Peter Proctor and Peter Harper (the famous 1961 Le Mans team). This was followed by a Nog and Natter and then Disco and Buffet in the Donington museum on the Saturday evening. The next morning, after every one had woken up, we held driving tests on the Melbourne Loop at Donington.

When the sun finally came out, we held a gymkhana. It's quite amazing what our members can be persuaded to do at these meetings. Richard Jones (our newsletter editor) is seen here during the skipping stage at the end of the course.

Undoubtedly, the biggest event on the U.K. motoring calendar is the Town and Country Motoring Festival (now known as the Ibcam Festival) held at Kenilworth, Warwickshire, over the August Bank Holiday week-end. The photo shows some of the S.A.O.C. members at our 1978 marquee display, just before the start of the event.

Donington is without doubt a terrific place to hold a club meeting, but unfortunately by 1979 they had increased their prices to extortionate levels, in what seemed an attempt to keep the clubs away. Certainly, all the club secretaries I have spoken to, who have in the past used Donington for their meetings, are hesitant to return. If anyone from Donington ever reads this, please note my comments! It does annoy me when I think that the one-make car clubs financed the legal fight to re-open and re-build Donington and now the owners seem to have turned their backs on them. One day, finances permitting, I would like to return, but at present I can find far more important things to spend the members' money on.

After our first national meeting, the next event the club attended was the 1978 *Thoroughbred and Classic Cars* Concours. This was followed by a new event, launched over the August Bank holiday weekend – the Town and Country Motoring Festival held at the Royal Agricultural Showground, Stoneleigh. In my opinion, this is one of the best motoring events held in the U.K. and I would urge any motoring enthusiast to give it a try. It's not just the largest motoring event of the season, but covers a wide variety of subjects from cattle shows to parachute displays. It was at this event that the S.A.O.C./Chrysler relationship took a turn for the

Ryton-on-Dunsmore, 1980: 21 years after the introduction of the Alpine, we returned to the old Rootes factory where it was made, now used by Talbot (U.K.) Ltd. for assembling the present-day Alpine. After a tour of the works and lunch, we held a motorcade through Coventry city centre, aided by the Warwickshire police force who did a fantastic job, keeping all the Alpines in one very long line.

better. The display we had put on attracted a great number of people, many of whom had worked for the Rootes Group in the past. Some had stayed on and now worked for Chrysler, and to our amazement a few turned out to be Chrysler managers and directors. From that moment on, the cooperation we received from Chrysler (and later, Talbot) could not have been better.

The number of events the club attends has increased each year and we can now offer a wide variety of activities, including 19 different monthly meetings.

1980 was a special year, being the 21st anniversary of the introduction of the Alpine. Together with the management of Talbot, we thought it only fitting that we should return to the place where the Alpines were made, the factory at Ryton-on-Dunsmore, to hold our celebrations in June. After a tour of the assembly lines where the current Talbot Alpine is produced, we all enjoyed a lunch provided by the management. We then took part in a motorcade organized in conjunction with the Warwickshire police force through the streets of Coventry, and finally a club concours judged by the directors of Talbot.

The club has not just concentrated its activities upon the events I have described. A great deal of time has been spent trying to locate obsolete spare parts or, where this is impossible, trying to have them remanufactured. As every Alpine owner knows, spares have become an increasing problem over the last few years, particularly since so many

The Ibcam Festival, 1979 — the marquee gets bigger and the display gets better. That year, we were placed sixth in the overall listing of club displays and came away with a large cheque. Many people gathered in the marquee to watch our almost continuous film shows of Alpines in rallies and at Le Mans.

owners now want to renovate their Alpines instead of scrapping them as in the past. But spares need not be a worry if the owner joins one of the clubs which caters for the Alpine. With the exception of body panels, nearly all the spares required for an Alpine can be obtained from one source or another: it is just a matter of knowing where. If they cannot be bought off the shelf or if the club does not have its own supply, the chances are they can be made up specially. Contrary to popular belief, one-offs do not cost the earth, and in fact I have found that it is usually cheaper to make spares than to buy them straight off the shelf.

The club itself has, over the last year or so, built up its own stocks of spares and has also embarked on a remanufacturing programme. I am only too willing to try to locate any spares needed by our members. If I am unable to track down any particular item (which is not that often, as I have excellent contacts in the trade), the club will consider having it manufactured. Parts which are necessary to keep the Alpines roadworthy take priority, of course, but we normally win in the end. Of course, not all spares can be made, due to cost, and some body fittings have caused concern in the past, but normally items from scrapped vehicles can be used quite adequately. If you own an Alpine and if you intend to keep it on the road, it is imperative that you join one of the clubs. They represent the only comprehensive source of spares, and in most clubs, spares are sold to members only. This is, of course, the biggest benefit the clubs can offer.

At the time I started to write this book, no body panels to speak of were available. One firm has been advertising some in the U.K. but I'm afraid I cannot possibly recommend them, for reasons best kept to myself. The club's search for a prospective manufacturer has thus continued and I do believe we may now have found one. I cannot give you full details at present as we have not had time to sort them out. I can tell you that this firm has started building prototype front wings for costing. This will be followed by door skins and probably rear wing repair sections. By the time this book is released the project should be in full swing (or abandoned), and as I keep in close touch with most of the clubs listed in this chapter, they will keep their members informed as to its progress.

What about the club's future? Apart from continuing our battle to find all the remaining spares and build up our manufacturing programme, several members are contemplating forming a racing team to enter in the Historic Sports Car Club events. I for one have already started to rebuild a Harrington 'D' type with this in mind.

I have always intended to expand the club by accepting all Rootes vehicles, as there are still a great number of models which are not catered for by any club. I have always felt that this would be a great advantage for everyone concerned. Who knows, one day this might happen and we may see a new club called the Rootes Owners Club.

Name of club	**SUNBEAM TIGER OWNERS CLUB**
Membership secretary	**Ray Murray**
Address	**25A The Drive, Ilford, Essex, IG1 3E2**
Number of members	**Over 300**
Vehicles eligible	**Tigers only**

The Sunbeam Tiger Owners Club was formed in 1975 with a nucleus of about 20 Tiger enthusiasts, and has continued to grow in membership, status and activity ever since.

About 7,000 Tigers were built at the Jensen factory in West Bromwich, between late 1964 and 1967, and exported in the main to the west coast of America, where it quickly became known as the California sun-shine car. About 800 were sold on the U.K. market, but it is believed that fewer than 400 survive today. It says a great deal for the S.T.O.C. that well over 300 of these belong to members of the club.

The S.T.O.C. has ambitious annual programmes that would do credit to much larger single marque clubs with memberships of many thousands. It holds regional monthly meetings in the Midlands and in the London area throughout the year. At least six national week-end meetings take place, usually at Post Houses in various centres round the country, between March and November. The Club's annual three-day holiday and concours event is held in Looe, Cornwall, on the last week-end in September. An informative and comprehensive club magazine is published quarterly. A trip abroad is organized for members every year; in 1980, thirty club members were hosted in California for the annual convention of Tigers.

While the Tiger shares the body panel problems of its sister, the Alpine, engine parts and modified high performance parts for the Fairline and Mustang V8 engine are readily available 'off the shelf' from American car stockists.

Name of club	**SUNBEAM AND TALBOT OWNERS CLUB**
Membership secretary	**Name not supplied**
Address	**Box 170, East Melbourne, Victoria, 3002, Australia**
Number of members	**36**
Number of Alpines on register	**23**
Vehicles eligible	**Any Sunbeams or Talbots**

The Sunbeam and Talbot Owners Club was formed in 1973, following a discussion between several Alpine owners at a concours run by the M.G. Car Club. An initial meeting was advertised and about 20 enthusiasts turned up, owning a variety of Sunbeams between them, ranging from a 1946 side valve saloon to Tigers.

The membership almost doubled over the years and a wide range of cars is still catered for, although Alpines are the most numerous. Possibly the most interesting car to pass through the club was one of the Le Mans Tigers. This car is still in Melbourne.

The club's activities include monthly meetings, rallies, concours, autokhanas, and social events. Some of these are held in conjunction with other one-make clubs. The last five years have seen annual meetings with Sunbeam clubs from other states during long weekends, and these have been very successful despite the distances involved.

Resources such as spares, information and a library are being actively built up and efforts are being made to track down as many owners as possible to ensure the club's continued progress and growth.

Name of Club	**SUNBEAM SPORTSCAR OWNERS CLUB OF CANADA**
Membership secretary	**Miss Anne Murray**

Address	Box 875, Station 'Q', Toronto, Ontario, Canada
Number of members	65
Number of Alpines on register	40
Vehicles eligible	Alpines and Tigers (full membership) Other Sunbeam models (associated membership)

Founded in September 1978, the club's membership is located mainly in Southern Ontario, concentrated on the Metropolitan Toronto area.

It holds rallies and meets on a regular basis, its two major fixed events being the spring meet, held the first Sunday after Victoria Day (May 24th), and the anniversary meet, held the closest Sunday to the founding date of 23rd September. After its first meeting, the club established contact with S.A.O.C. in the U.K. and the New Zealand Sunbeam Club, and this has been maintained on a regular basis. It also liaizes with Tigers East/Alpines East in the U.S.A.

The club publishes a bi-monthly newsletter containing articles about members and their cars, and including an article for Tiger owners, want ads, and technical tips. It has its own constitution, badge, and a yearly elected executive board.

Name of club	NEW ZEALAND SUNBEAM OWNERS CLUB
Membership secretary	Barry Hammond
Address	P.O. Box 1445, Hamilton, New Zealand
Number of members	83
Number of Alpines on register	20
Vehicles eligible	All Sunbeams

Founded in 1972, the club was originally mainly orientated towards the Sunbeam Rapier, the 3A model of 1961–3 being the most prevalent. Since then, it has grown to around 80 members, many of whom own Alpines, which are considered to be very much the 'in thing' to have by the New Zealand 'sports car set'. The club now has four branches in New Zealand and is looking towards forming more. It holds an annual general meeting in August which incorporates a hotly contested concours. It also plans to include a short navigation rally in 1980. Other events include economy runs, concours, navigation runs, pub nights, runs to places of interest, service days, valet days and film shows. The club has a strong social side as well, and tries to combine social activities with motoring events wherever possible.

Since its last A.G.M., the club has established a spare parts scheme which is slowly turning up some useful spares – though not in great quantity, as the number of Sunbeams imported to New Zealand was relatively small.

The club enjoys hearing from fellow Sunbeamers overseas and particularly appreciates other club magazines. Enthusiasts in New Zealand have backed the Sunbeam marque for some time and are naturally delighted that the movement is at last gathering steam in Britain and the U.S.A.!

Name of Club	**SUNBEAM SPORTS CAR CLUB OF SOUTH AFRICA**
Membership secretary	**Willie Cronje**
Address	**P.O. Box 203, Oudtshoorn, 6620, South Africa**
Number of members	**50**
Number of Alpines on register	**36**
Vehicles eligible	**Mainly Alpines and Tigers, but enquire if you own any other type of Sunbeam**

This club was started in November 1978, with nine members mainly based in Capetown, while the Secretary lived in Oudtshoorn, 250 miles from

The South African town of Parow celebrates its 75th anniversary, and the Sunbeam Alpine Club of South Africa provides the 18 carnival finalists with suitable means of transport. (S.A.C.S.A.).

The real thing in miniature. This beautifully made replica of a Sunbeam Alpine was made by three of the staff of a garage in Lourenco Marques, Mozambique, East Africa, for the 7-year-old son of a local doctor. It took 18 months to build, has lights, radio, horn and direction indicators, and its petrol engine gives it a speed of between 25 and 30 m.p.h.

Capetown. Its main activities are breakfast runs and Sunday outings. Originally called 'The Sunbeam Alpine Club' its name was changed to 'The Sunbeam Sports Car Club' because of the shortage of Alpines – and requests from Tiger owners who wished to join. The club issues a very informative newsletter called *The Sunbeam Voice*.

Name of Club	**SUNBEAM OWNERS CLUB OF SWEDEN**
Membership secretary	**Johnny Arksund**
Address	**Korsgatan 13, S-244 02 Furulund, Sweden**
Number of members	95
Number of Alpines on register	95
Eligible vehicles	**All Rootes Group Vehicles**

The club was formed in 1977 to assist owners of all Rootes Group marques to maintain and preserve their vehicles.

The club arranges two national meetings every summer, and monthly area meetings in some parts of the country. It also publishes a club magazine, the *Sunbeam Post*, four times yearly.

The club holds a stock of spares for most cars in the Rootes Group, and sells club items such as stickers, badges and 'T' shirts. It also runs a parts remanufacturing programme.

Name of club	**SUNBEAM OWNERS ASSOCIATION**
Membership secretary	**Richard T. Trenk Sr.**
Address	**13568 W. Mississippi Court, Lakewood, Colorado, 80228, U.S.A.**
Number of members	**150**
Number of Alpines on register	**197**
Vehicles eligible	**Sunbeams**

The club was founded in 1972 by Richard Trenk, for the benefit of Alpine owners in Colorado and surrounding regions.

Activities are limited to technical seminars and social gatherings in the Denver area, although some joint participation with other clubs in sponsoring rallies is planned for the future. The club's primary purpose, however, is to provide technical and spares support to Alpine and Tiger owners.

Richard Trenk operates the club in conjunction with his Sunbeam repair garage, R.P.M. Ltd., situated in Lakewood. He also races a Series 5 Alpine in S.C.C.A. road racing contests.

Name of club	**SUNBEAM CAR CLUB OF AMERICA**
Membership secretary	**Joe Lewis**
Address	**592 Baron Street, Toms River, N.J. 08753, U.S.A.**
Number of members	**580**
Number of Alpines on register	**435**
Vehicles eligible	**Any Rootes Group vehicle**

This club was formed in May 1976 as the first all Sunbeam marque club in the United States. For many years, owners of Sunbeams and other Rootes Group vehicles have known the frustrations of hard-to-find, costly or simply unavailable parts, improper technical assistance and a general lack of support from the automotive accessory manufacturers. The purpose of the club is to change all that. Its aim is to promote the restoration,

The Sunbeam Car Club of America: just some of the members that turned out for one of the club's meetings. (S.C.C.A.)

technical maintenance and general appreciation of the Rootes Group marques, by acting as a source of information, encouraging the gathering of members and providing events for the enjoyment of the owners.

The club publishes a newsletter called *On The Beam* six times yearly, covering marque history, technical tips, swap and shop, and news of members and club events.

As the club is organized in conjunction with a firm called Classic Sunbeam Auto Parts, which is run by the membership secretary and the club president Curt Meinel, it has a strong parts reproduction programme. Details are included in the newsletter.

Name of club	**SUNBEAM ALPINE CLUB**
Membership secretary	**Rush Bash**
Address	**1752 Oswald Place, Santa Clara, Calif. 95050, U.S.A.**
Number of members	**200**
Number of Alpines on register	**250**
Vehicles eligible	**Alpines**

The club was founded in 1978 with six members. It now meets every month to have picnics, swap parts, demonstrate mechanical repairs and tune-ups, admire each other's cars, exchange information relating to obtaining spare parts or reasonable repairs, go on tours, visit race tracks and wineries, enter rallies, and Autocross events – in fact, the usual car club activities. Occasionally, meetings are combined with those of the Tiger Club or an all-British car club.

The club has a monthly newsletter, which shares information with out of town members who can't always attend meetings. The news includes reports of previous activities, upcoming events, articles on technical repairs or various problems, authorized reprints from road and track magazines regarding the Alpine, want ads., cameo articles on interesting members and their cars, and occasional lewd pictures which the editor insists upon printing, in spite of severe condemnation by the club's president, secretary and treasurer.

Name of club	**CALIFORNIA ASSOCIATION OF TIGER OWNERS**
Membership secretary	**Chuck Daly**
Address	**4508 El Reposo Drive, Eagle Rock, Calif. 90065, U.S.A.**
Number of members	**800 plus**
Number of Alpines on register	**Not supplied**
Vehicles eligible	**Alpines and Tigers**

Elizabeth Taylor and her Alpine in the film 'Human Jungle'.

The club's beginning was simple, when a small group of people gathered together ten years ago to exchange ideas, and form a social group. Today C.A.T. is a strong viable club with more than 800 members throughout the world, and still growing.

Its monthly newspaper, *Tiger Tales*, contains articles pertaining to the club's monthly meetings and includes a classified section in which members may find or sell a car, and a shopnote section containing valuable information with respect to answering some of those not too often answerable questions, along with general fix-it information.

Discounts are available on various items such as Lat valve covers, Lat hoods, flares, windshields, carpet kits, mag wheels, sway bars, soft tops, all rubber mouldings, springs, brake hoses, heavy duty radiators, headers, exhaust systems, and much more. Most parts are stocked in C.A.T.'s own warehouse for distribution to club members.

New technical innovations, such as spin on-off oil filters, suspension systems and quick steering units, are now available at substantial savings to C.A.T. members. In addition, the club has recently published a complete anthology of shop notes generated over the past ten years. This 250-page manual is an invaluable tool for anyone working on a Tiger, containing information on all aspects of car care, maintenance and performance enhancements. These manuals are available to all club members.

The club is able to locate many parts which it does not carry in stock. Some hard-to-find items may take a while, but it can usually track them down or suggest an alternative part that will do the job. C.A.T. is also into manufacturing parts such as Lat Options, all rubber mouldings, and Tiger script insignia.

Name of Club	**SUNBEAM TIGER OWNERS PACIFIC**
Membership secretary	**Terrence Chun**
Address	**P.O. Box 561, Honolulu, H.I. 96809**
Number of members	**12**
Number of Alpines on register	**8**
Vehicles eligible	**Alpines and Tigers**

This club was started in the fall of 1976 by a handful of Sunbeam Tiger owners, hence the name 'Sunbeam Tiger Owners Pacific'. Due to their distance from the mainland and limited membership, they decided to become affiliated with the Sunbeam Tiger Owners Association in the San Francisco Bay area.

A scene from the Jack Cummings production 'Bachelor Flat', released by 20th Century Fox.

Their club has expanded to include Alpines as well, primarily because many of the technical tips and advice on parts suppliers are equally applicable to both Tiger and Alpine owners. Due to the Aloha extended by the Sunbeam Car Club of America, Tigers/Alpines East and the California Association of Tiger Owners via their parts suppliers and technical tips, they are able to obtain for members the benefits of membership in essentially five car clubs.

Among their activities are tours, autocrossing, rallying, car shows, fix-ins and, of course, preservation, restoration and in some cases improvements and/or modifications, depending on personal tastes. As an aside, the president won the 1978 B.P. Class S.C.C.A. Autocrossing Championship in his 1965 Tiger.

Name of Club	**PACIFIC TIGER CLUB**
Membership secretary	**Kevin Jewell**
Address	**14705 NE 64th Redmond, W.A. 98052, U.S.A.**
Number of members	**28**
Number of Alpines in register	**16**
Vehicles eligible	**Alpines and Tigers**

The Pacific Tiger Club is composed of active Tiger and/or Alpine owners, several members owning both marques. While the club does print its own newsletter, it does not manufacture or sell parts as a club, nor does it encourage non-local members. This is basically an activity club, most members joining in order to partake of group activities such as autocrossing, rallying, touring and concoursing.

Appendices

I Road Test Reports

'The Motor' Road Test Number 29/59 (Continental)
Published in 'The Motor' – 18th November 1959
Make: SUNBEAM ALPINE, SERIES 1 (with Overdrive)

Test Conditions
Weather: hot and dry with light breeze
Temperature: 67°–77°
Barometer: 29.9–30.0 in H.G.
Dry concrete and tarmac surfaces.

Weight
Kerb weight (with oil, water and fuel for approx. 50 miles):   19½ cwt.
Front – rear distribution per cent: 51/49
Laden as tested: 23¼ cwt.

Turning Circles
Between kerbs: L–33¼ ft;   R–34¾ ft.
Turns of steering wheel lock to lock: 3.5

Performance Data
Overdrive top gear m.p.h. per 1000 r.p.m.:   20–2
Top gear m.p.h. per 1000 r.p.m.:   16–2
Mean piston speed at max. power: 2,650 ft./min.
Engine revs. at mean max speed: 5,300 r.p.m.

Fuel: Premium grade (96 octane r.m.)
Test distance: 2,721 miles
Overall fuel consumption: 27.4 m.p.g.
Normal range: not given
Oil: S.A.E. 20
Oil consumption: 2,000 miles per pint

Acceleration Times in Seconds (Upper Gears Only)

	overdrive top gear	top gear	overdrive 3rd gear	third gear
10–30 m.p.h.	—	10.8	9.6	7.7
20–40 m.p.h.	14.6	10.2	9.6	6.8
30–50 m.p.h.	14.9	9.9	8.3	6.2
40–60 m.p.h.	15.8	10.3	8.6	6.9
50–70 m.p.h.	17.3	10.9	9.5	8.8
60–80 m.p.h.	21.0	13.5	12.2	11.8
70–90 m.p.h.	29.5	17.1	—	—

Acceleration Times (in Seconds) From Standstill

0–30	4.9
0–40	7.0
0–50	10.2
0–60	13.6
0–70	17.9
0–80	24.7
0–90	35.0
Standing $\frac{1}{4}$ mile	19.7

Brakes

	pedal load	retardation	equiv. distance
From 30 m.p.h.	70 lb.	0.91 g.	33 ft.
	50 lb.	0.60 g.	50 ft.
	25 lb.	0.30 g.	100 ft.

Fuel Consumption (Constant Speeds on Level)

	m.p.g. overdrive top gear	m.p.g. direct top gear
30 m.p.h.	46.0	41.5
40 m.p.h.	45.0	40.0
50 m.p.h.	39.5	35.0
60 m.p.h.	35.0	31.0
70 m.p.h.	31.0	28.0
80 m.p.h.	27.5	23.0
90 m.p.h.	24.5	—

The Sunbeam Alpine (with overdrive)

Introduced during the summer as a completely new model, the Sunbeam Alpine which we have been able to test in England, Belgium, France, Germany and Switzerland, combines in a single competitively priced car some of the best of two worlds. Eye-catching sports car lines are matched by the brisk acceleration, the maximum speed of virtually 100 m.p.h., highly responsive steering and reassuringly powerful disc brakes. But if this is a sports car, it belongs to the new generation of sports cars which is not merely weatherproof when required, but offers two people greater comfort than they would enjoy in many quite expensive touring cars.

It is no secret that the competitive price of this model (including purchase tax, it only exceeds £1,000 when extras such as the overdrive are added to its basic specification) is possible because the design takes advantage of tooling which has been laid down for other Rootes Group models; the power unit has a basic similarity to Hillman and Singer

'Eye catching sports car lines are matched by the brisk acceleration, the maximum speed of virtually 100 m.p.h., highly responsive steering and reassuringly powerful disc brakes.'

units, and the chassis uses some Husky estate car pressings in its make-up. Consequently, it is pleasing to be able to record at the end of an extended trial that certain characteristics which have recently been noted almost as 'family failings' seem to have been eradicated. Oil consumption on this car was so small, for example, that the Alpine ran nearly 2,000 miles in our hands before any excuse could be found for topping up the engine sump with a single pint. Gearbox ratios which used to earn almost automatic criticism have given place to ratios whose spacing should please anyone who is not actually allergic to gear levers. Handling qualities far more sensitive and responsive than might have been expected have been built into this model. Despite a higher compression ratio than has been used on any former Rootes engine, this car with its new aluminium cylinder head (in which no two exhaust valves adjoin one another) is happy even on the not-very-good petrol of France.

Scaling not very far short of one ton in convertible form (it is easy to add a rigid 'hard top' without removing the folded hood) this 1½ litre car has too much strength and comfort built into it to offer 'racing' acceleration, but it will perform well for two different kinds of driver. In sporting mood, and using the overdrive and the four gearbox ratios freely to let the engine get up to and beyond 5,000 r.p.m. quite frequently, a keen driver gets over the ground very fast indeed to the tune of a hearty bark from the exhaust. More sedately driven and perhaps with the overdrive switch used as a lazy man's substitute for the gear lever, the

Alpine still gets over the ground quite quickly and with a lot less exhaust noise, the engine being perfectly willing to pull away from 1,000 r.p.m. in one of the higher gears, but its torque rising gradually over much of the speed range at a rate which in top gear roughly matches the car's rise in air resistance, so that top gear acceleration remains remarkably constant in rate from 10 m.p.h. right up to 70 m.p.h.

With such a versatile engine, there were naturally wide variations in fuel consumption according to where and how the Alpine was driven, our worst figure over a substantial distance being 19.4 m.p.g. when hard-driving members of the staff sampled the car in and near to London, our best reading 32.2 m.p.g. during a fairly leisurely exploration of Black Forest mountain roads. The fuel tank capacity of this model is nominally 9 gallons, but a gauge which indicated an emphatic zero when 7 gallons had been used out of a brim-full tank discouraged long drives without refuelling.

Our test car had the Laycock de Normanville switch-controlled overdrive as a very welcome supplement to the four speed gearbox, operative in conjunction with top or third gears, and smooth in engagement yet free from slip at all times; in conjunction with the overdrive a 4.222 axle ratio gives livelier top gear acceleration than the 3.889 ratio otherwise specified. For sheer maximum speed, the combination used for our test may not be ideal, 5,600 r.p.m. (the red mark on the tachometer dial, and a speed beyond which the valvegear becomes suddenly very noisy) representing 91 m.p.h. in direct top gear but the timed maximum of 99.5 m.p.h. in overdrive top gear being short of the 5,300 r.p.m. at which maximum power is developed. For anything other than level-road maximum speed, however, the overdrive obviously much improves the car, there being a 'right' ratio available for acceleration over any possible speed range, and a sustained 80 m.p.h. on daylong Autobahn drives seeming effortless and quite economical at only 4,000 r.p.m.

An extremely pleasant central remote control is provided for this model's silent new four-speed gearbox, which has quite good synchromesh on gears other than 1st. Overdrive 3rd is a ratio only slightly lower than direct top gear (at 5,000 r.p.m. one gives 72 m.p.h. and the other 81 m.p.h.) and is used very frequently, in town for quiet progress at 30 m.p.h. or on the open road when regaining cruising speed.

X-braced amidships and with the scuttle structure linked to the i.f.s. anchorages by tubular struts, the Alpine's integral body chassis structure appears notably rigid, cobbled Flanders by-ways causing no evident distorting – something which it is rarely possible to say about an open car with wide doors. The springing is soft enough for pavé to cause no

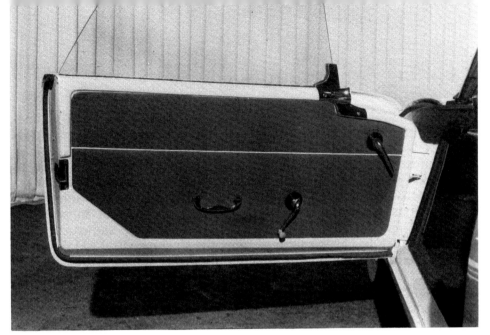

'The Alpine's integral body chassis structure appears notably rigid, cobbled Flanders by-ways causing no evident distorting — something which it is rarely possible to say about an open car with wide doors.'

discomfort whatever, even with the Dunlop 'Road Speed' tyres at the higher inflation pressures advised for fast motorway cruising, and some buyers might actually prefer rather firmer damping of the springs. It is low build and reasonable track width which let this car corner quickly with very little body roll, and not the use of harsh spring. Really pushed towards the limit on a bumpy corner, the Alpine's rear axle can begin to hop somewhat under its semi-elliptic springs, but general standards of road holding are high.

In respect of steering this car invites judgement by far higher standards than any other recent Rootes car, a driver soon learning that he can relax physically and guide the car with finger pressures on the wheel rim at most times. There is feel in the steering but not any tiring amount of reaction from bumpy roads, the further improvement which might be welcome being closer harmony between fairly strong castor and understeer when the car is cornering and an almost excessive degree of steering sensitivity during fast driving along a straight road. Despite the vestigial tail fins formed by the rear wings, the car yields noticeably to wind rather than 'weathercocking' towards it, but with correctly matched front and rear tyre pressures this is a car which makes fast progress along reasonably traffic-free roads a real joy.

In making notes about the Alpine, it was afterwards realized that all reference to the brakes had been completely omitted, which for a rapid and hard-driven car is a silent testimony to their excellence. Disc brakes behind the bolt-on front wheels work with the drum-type rear brakes to give all the braking which is required or which road adhesion permits, quietly and in response to a comfortably moderate pedal pressure, whilst the hand-brake can hold the car on a 1 in 3 gradient.

Amenities for the driver and passenger in the Alpine are centred on two bucket seats; their upholstery is reasonably firm but the standard of comfort provided on a long journey is far higher than on the superficially soft cushions (providing little or no lateral support) of most family saloons. Since the first batch of Alpines went into showrooms, the steering column has been raised to bring the steering wheel rim clear of a driver's thighs, and the driving position of our test model made people of very varied shapes and sizes comfortable. At first acquaintance, headroom when the hood is erect seems limited and a piece of hood-frame is rather near to a tall driver's head, but the car is so sprung that proximity never becomes contact.

Whereas most sporting cars which can be compared in price with the Alpine use removable sidescreens, and can gain elbow width by having hollowed-out or cutaway doors, this model has wind-down glass windows. In respect of weather-proofness, clear vision and general convenience this is obviously an advantageous arrangement. At first acquaintance, a bulky driver is conscious that his shoulder readily contacts the door, but tumble-home on the body sides provides extra width at elbow level, even more width at floor level so that a very convenient pull-up handbrake lever can be accommodated on the driver's off side. Erect, the side windows seal against rubber strips on the windscreen frame, and lowered they disappear completely from view, but a tendency for the hood sides to suck outwards at speeds over 60 m.p.h. can interfere with the complete closing of an opened window.

Separate from the spare wheel stowage, the lockable rear luggage compartment has a flat floor which will not harm cases, but is too shallow be very capacious. A large well behind the front seats provides a great deal more carrying capacity, and a passenger sitting sideways can travel here. Extra accommodation under lock and key is provided inside what appear to be only an armrest (and a very useful one) between the front seats.

As an open car, the Alpine has no visible trace of any hood. Three hinged metal covers painted to match the rest of the coachwork conceal both fabric and framework. As a closed car, there is full protection against draught and rain, but a fair amount of 'wind whistle' which builds up as the cruising speed goes beyond 70 m.p.h. and on a motorway, demands rather a high volume from the loud speaker if a radio programme is to be enjoyed. As always, practice allows the job to be done more quickly and more neatly, but neither erection of the hood

'A large well behind the front seats provides a great deal more carrying capacity, and a passenger sitting sideways can travel here.'

'As an open car, the Alpine has no visible trace of any hood. Three-hinged metal covers painted to match the rest of the coachwork conceal both fabric and framework.'

nor its neat stowage in the wells provided are particularly rapid though both jobs are entirely practicable single-handed. A further nuisance for well-laden holiday makers is that the hood covers will not hinge open fully unless the rear 'seat' is cleared of luggage. A parcel compartment of substantial size on the facia, with a lip which holds maps and guide-books in position, helps tourists to keep their car reasonably tidy.

Equipment on this car lets both the sporting motorist and the sybarite enjoy it. The former has a neat and legible set of instruments, including oil pressure gauge, coolant thermometer, trip speedometer, rev. counter and provision for an ammeter if desired; a good all-round view kept clear by windscreen washing sprays, and convenient controls which include a horn ring. The latter can have a heater to supplement the fresh-air ventilation system, will appreciate doors wide enough to make this amongst the easiest of low-built cars to enter, and can relax thanks to the vibration-free engine and shock-free springing.

A dual appeal is, in fact, the essence of the Alpine. For young people who want a sports car but need accommodation for one or two small children, it can satisfy both the wish and the need at reasonable cost.

'Equipment on this car lets both the sporting motorist and the sybarite enjoy it.'

Anyone of an older generation whose family have grown up and bought their own cars, and who is getting bored with driving on crowded roads, should consider whether perhaps a comfortable yet nimble car such as the Alpine is not perhaps the 'prescription' for putting pleasure back into motoring.

'Autocar' Road Test Number 1860
Published in 'Autocar' – 16th February 1962
Make: SUNBEAM HARRINGTON LE MANS (1592 c.c.)
Manufacturer: Thomas Harrington Ltd., Sackville Works, Old Shoreham Road, Hove, Sussex

Test Conditions
Weather: cold and damp with 10 m.p.h. wind
Temperature: 34° F. (1° C.)
Barometer: 29.6 in. H.G.
Damp concrete and tarmac surfaces.

Weight
Kerb weight (with oil, water and half-full fuel tank):   2,275 lb.
Front – rear distribution, per cent: F–50-1; R–49-9
Laden as tested: 2,611 lb.

Turning Circles
Between kerbs: L–32 ft. 11 ins.;   R–34 ft. 3 ins.
Between walls: L–34 ft. 3 ins.;   R–35 ft. 7 ins.
Turns of steering wheel lock to lock: 3.5

Performance Data
Overdrive top gear m.p.h. per 1000 r.p.m.:   19.75
Top gear m.p.h. per 1000 r.p.m.:   15.9
Mean piston speed at max. power: 3,000 ft./min.
Engine revs. at mean max. speed: 5,100 r.p.m.
B.h.p. per ton laden: 82.3

Fuel: Super Premium grade (100 octane r.m.)
Test distance: 1,002 miles
Overall consumption: 20.1 m.p.g.
Normal range: 20–30 m.p.g.
Oil: S.A.E. 10W30
Oil consumption: 7,500 m.p.g.

Speed Range and Time in Seconds
(First gear without overdrive not tested)

m.p.h.	o/d top	top	o/d third	third	o/d second	second	o/d first
10–30	—	—	—	8.6	6.3	5.0	3.5
20–40	—	—	10.9	7.3	5.1	4.0	—
30–50	20.6	10.9	9.5	7.0	5.5	—	—
40–60	19.6	10.9	9.6	6.0	—	—	—
50–70	18.0	11.3	10.0	—	—	—	—
60–80	21.0	13.1	12.0	—	—	—	—
70–90	28.9	17.2	—	—	—	—	—

Acceleration Times (in Seconds) From Standstill

30 m.p.h.	4.5
40 m.p.h.	6.5
50 m.p.h.	9.0
60 m.p.h.	13.0
70 m.p.h.	17.6
80 m.p.h.	24.8
90 m.p.h.	37.4
Standing $\frac{1}{4}$ mile	19.3

Brakes

	pedal load	retardation	equiv. distance
From 30 m.p.h. in neutral	25 lb.	0.34 g.	89 ft.
	50 lb.	0.72 g.	41 ft.
	75 lb.	0.93 g.	32.5 ft.
Handbrake		0.40 g.	75 ft.

Fuel Consumption (Constant Speeds on Level)

m.p.h.	m.p.g. overdrive top gear	m.p.g. direct top gear
30	45	43
40	49	40
50	43	38
60	36	33
70	32	28
80	28	25
90	24	—

Sunbeam Harrington Le Mans 1,592 c.c.

More than one firm that is now internationally famous started life by adapting a current production car to suit its own ideas. Thomas

'The glass-fibre fixed-head coupé roof is no temporary hard top, and the rear runs down smoothly to where the tail is cut sharply away.'

Harrington Ltd., of Hove, have been coachbuilders for many years, but it is less than 12 months since this concern announced the first of its restyled Rootes Sunbeam Alpines. A test of one of these was published in *Autocar* of 23rd June 1961.

At just about this time a new prototype body appeared and was fitted to one of the Alpines which ran in the Le Mans 24-hour race; this car won the Index of Thermal Efficiency. Harrington decided to go into production with this body, and the car was introduced at the Earls Court Motor Show, and named the Le Mans after its race success.

Abroad, the Rootes Export Division will look after sales and servicing of the Sunbeam Harrington which only very recently has been introduced to the United States.

Back as far as the windscreen pillars and the doors, construction is pure Sunbeam Alpine; considerable alterations have been made to the rest of the car. The glass-fibre fixed-head coupé roof is no temporary hard top, and the rear runs down smoothly to where the tail is cut sharply away. Removal of the tail fins allows the rear wings to blend in smoothly with the line of the roof. Clusters of rear lamps on the cut-off back replace those previously mounted in the fins. A good-sized luggage door with an interior catch includes the large rear window and replaces the small boot lid.

Inside the car, the normal seats have been replaced by well-made and shaped Microcell bucket seats. Behind them there are two minute

'Back as far as the windscreen pillars and the doors, construction is pure Sunbeam Alpine; considerable alterations have been made to the rest of the car.'

optional seats, but more important is the fact that the backrest for these folds forward to provide a greatly extended luggage platform. With this squab down, the total length of the luggage compartment is 46 in. It has considerable depth, so that for a two-seater touring car the Le Mans is well supplied with luggage space. Beneath this compartment, and reached by lifting a trap door directly below the rear window, are the spare wheel, jack and other tools. This area was not waterproof, and in wet weather a quantity of water collected here.

These are the body alterations that Harrington have carried out; quality of workmanship is commendable, and the glass-fibre roof is well made and free from movement. In fact, it appears to be an integral part of the original body. One small complaint was that certain road surfaces, notably concrete ones, produced a high-pitched and irritating resonance in the roof. Wind roar was almost entirely absent but the car was never completely free from road noise.

The quality of the car suffers from an original shortcoming; just over a year ago, the Sunbeam Alpine Mark 2 which was road tested by *Autocar* leaked badly through the floor and round the leading edge of the door. This car suffered from exactly the same trouble.

Plenty of headroom is provided, and the driving position is good. A driver approaching six feet in height had insufficient leg and particularly arm room for real comfort, but it would not be difficult to move the seat runners a little further back. For the passenger, a slightly less upright squab would be more comfortable and relaxing.

Engine Modifications

The increase in price over the normal Alpine does not merely include these body alterations but also a moderately high degree of tuning to the engine. The small extra weight penalty that this body work entails is more than compensated for by increased power; the engine modifications are carried out by George Hartwell Ltd., of Bournemouth, a firm which has had many years' experience of tuning these power units. Modifications to the engine include a new camshaft, reshaping of the inlet and exhaust ports, and a change of choke and jet sizes in the two down-draught Zenith carburettors. These alterations, it is claimed, raise the power output from 80 b.h.p. at 5,000 r.p.m. to 96 b.h.p. at 6,000 r.p.m. This, however, must be a purely theoretical figure, since the point of valve crash is reached well below this engine speed at 5,800 r.p.m.

One of the impressions given by this power unit, and for that matter by certain minor features of the car, was lack of preparation. When delivered for test the engine would not tick over, and there seemed to be a distinct lack of crispness. Below about 2,000 r.p.m. there was little pulling power; indeed, there was such a bad flat spot that rapid opening of the throttle resulted in deceleration rather than the reverse. This absence of low-speed pulling power was probably the most unattractive feature of the car and certainly spoilt its potential as a tractable touring conveyance. On the other hand, there was a distinct improvement in performance over the normal Alpine.

Most marked increase in performance was at the top end of the scale; 90 m.p.h. could be reached 13 sec. quicker than with the standard Alpine, and a standing quarter-mile took nearly 0.5 sec. less time. Except for two factors, the standing start performance figures could almost certainly be improved. Rear axle tramp initially restricted the engine speed at which getaways could be made, and as the competition clutch warmed up it began to slip. This complaint became sufficiently bad for it to be necessary to ease well back on the throttle when making upward gear changes.

A further modification is the extension of the overdrive to work on all four forward speeds, which gave an option of eight ratios from which to choose. In obtaining the acceleration figures from standstill, overdrive bottom was ignored but in all the other gears the extra ratio was used. When in a hurry on twisty roads this wide range of gears allowed the engine speed to be kept well within the power range. Many owners would probably find this surfeit of gears a nuisance, and willingly exchange it for a wider power range.

When cold the engine would start instantly with a little choke that could be dispensed with almost immediately. It took some time to warm up and would repeatedly stall, whereupon it would not restart anything like so readily.

An overall fuel consumption of 20.1 m.p.g. was a shade worse than with the normal Alpine, but this was not surprising for a number of reasons. There was the stalling, the idling speed was fast in order to make the engine tick over at all, and in order to overcome the flat spot at slow speeds it was necessary to jab the throttle and accordingly work the accelerator pump. On the open road, however, it showed itself to have reasonable economy and for most main road runs a consumption around the 25 m.p.g. mark was recorded. For those not in a hurry, a figure better than 30 m.p.g. would not be too optimistic to hope for. Readers may have noticed in the graph showing fuel consumption at constant speeds that at 30 m.p.h. in overdrive top the consumption is higher than at 40 m.p.h. in the same gear. Without any doubt the reason for this was the unwillingness of the engine to run at such a slow speed in this gear, when it was near snatch-point the whole time.

With a nine-gallon fuel tank and no reserve, the touring range is rather limited. The small diameter filler cap would accept only a gentle flow from a filling station fuel pump without blowing back.

Assisted by a Clayton-Dewandre servo unit, the brakes on this car were excellent. A pedal load of 75 lb. resulted in a 0.93 g stop, but of even more importance was the fact that a mere 25 lb. pedal load gave a retardation of 0.34 g. Even on rather damp roads, a figure of 0.85 g (at 65 lb. pedal load) without wheel lock was recorded, which says much for the balance of this particular model. One feature previously noted on Alpines was apparent also on this car; after a few miles on wet roads the first brake application resulted in little initial retardation and then a tendency to pull to one side or the other as the braking power returned.

No adjustments have been made to the suspension, and the handling of this car would have been greatly enhanced by stiffer rear dampers. As it was, any unevenness in the road made the rear axle hop, and on at least one occasion the car was thrown sufficiently far sideways to cause embarrassment to a lorry being overtaken. Disregarding this waywardness of the rear end, the car has distinct understeer characteristics. During the time it was on test, there were several opportunities to try it on snow and ice. Rear wheel adhesion and traction under these conditions were not ideal with the car unladen, nor was throttle control helped by slight stickiness and the need to be fairly heavy footed to get any response at slow speeds.

On a saloon car the steering would be considered very good, but it is not quite up to the quality of a moderately expensive Grand Touring car.

There are $3\frac{1}{2}$ turns from lock to lock, and steering is light at all times although at slow speeds the wheel needs considerable movement.

The optional size tyres, 5.90 × 13 Dunlop RS5s, were fitted to this car, and it was found better to have them inflated rather hard, at 32 p.s.i., since at lower pressures the car's handling became somewhat uncertain and jelly-like in feel. Better handling at the higher pressures is, therefore, won at some sacrifice to the ride, which could not be described as soft. There was also a certain amount of roll, but the secure hold afforded by the bucket seats made this almost indiscernible.

Good Visibility
Visibility has not been impaired by the new roof, for the rear quarter vents run well aft and the rear window is large. The seating position is high and the view forward over the bonnet very complete. Most of the driving controls are well placed, except that the overdrive switch mounted on the steering column is located too close to the steering wheel itself, and could very easily be knocked in or out of action – an accident that could result in mechanical disaster. A horn-operating lever that is actuated by pushing it in any direction was often blown

'Most of the driving controls are well placed ... Instrumentation is to normal Alpine specification, and very adequate.'

inadvertently when reaching for the windscreen wiper switch. Absence of a headlamp flasher on this type and price of car is becoming less excusable. Replacement of the normal flat, sharp edged knob on the gear selector by a smooth pear-drop shaped wooden one has vastly improved the feel of this control. There is a wood-rimmed, alloy-spoked steering wheel and the sun vizors are of the soft safety-type. A lockable lid is provided for the facia glove pocket.

Instrumentation is to normal Alpine specification, and very adequate. Many of the instruments are graduated in both British and Continental scales.

During the bitter weather that heralded 1962 it was possible to draw very definite opinions about the heating system. The interior of the car became pleasantly warm, but the built-in extractors at the rear were not sufficient and to prevent the interior becoming stuffy one of the rear quarter-vents needed to be open. The windscreen could be kept demisted but the defroster could not start to cope with the conditions that are only

Only the early Harringtons Le Mans cars included vents to the rear of the back quarter light; as production progressed, they were omitted.

too common in many parts of North America. The rear window also tended to mist up.

This car was fitted with earless safety-type knock-off hubs, and a puncture that occurred during the test revealed that only a few wheel changes with the spanner provided would result in a badly mauled edge to the chromed nut. Secondly, the jack and jack handle, which appeared not to have been used previously, could not be persuaded to fit each other.

Down the inside of the doors is a thickly padded wedge which is designed to act as both an armrest and knee pad; in practice few who drove the car found it an advantage and it hindered easy operation of the window winders and door handles.

In conception the idea of the Harrington Le Mans appears to be absolutely right, and certain continental makes have shown that there is a large market for high quality, fast, two and occasional four-seater cars. Where it has lived up to its ideals the car is very pleasant, but it is a compromise between different designs and standards. Regardless of this, there is no doubt that its specification and quality will suit many tastes. This particular car tested showed signs of having had a hard life, and in good fettle some of the minor criticism probably would not apply.

Jack Brabham, Twice World Champion, Tests the
SERIES 3 ALPINE
Published in 'Modern Motoring and Travel' April 1963
Titled: This Is a Friendly Car

It seems only yesterday that I was trying out a Sunbeam Alpine round the tremendously fast Avus track in Berlin before the 1959 German Grand Prix. And now I have just been trying out the new Series 3 Alpine. This time the test had to be done between coming back from the Australian Grand Prix in Sydney, and flying back again to the other side of the world for a race at Longford, in Tasmania. But since I had to be in Coventry I took the opportunity of calling in at the Rootes factory at Ryton to see the new model.

I should really say models, for there are two versions of the Series 3 – the sports tourer and the Gran Turismo model.

In producing the Alpine G.T. the aim has been to give the customer even greater refinement in this sporty machine. To this end the engine has a different exhaust manifold and air cleaner, which reduces the sound level.

It also has a very neat and practical hardtop – and by practical I mean that you can sit in the car without knocking the top of your head off!

'In producing the Alpine G.T., the aim has been to give the customer even greater refinement in this sporty machine.'

Unlike some hard tops the Alpine G.T. has a generous measure of glass, and the rear window is large enough for the driver to see perfectly through the rear mirror (which is something I cannot say of some sports cars I have driven).

Other standard equipment on the G.T. includes carpeting instead of rubber floor covering, twin sun visors, courtesy light, a different rear quarter treatment, upholstered rear seat cushion, wood veneer facia, wood-rimmed steering wheel and heater. This turns it into a very complete motor car, and its refinement will surely tempt many a customer who wants good performance without any suggestion of roughing it.

At first glance I didn't think there were many changes. There is a new hood on the sports tourer (which is easier to operate than the former design, and which, in conjunction with the new seating, gives more headroom), fixed quarter lights at the front of the door windows, and a new badge carrying the series number. That, as far as I could see, was the full list of obvious differences – until I got into the car, drove it, and talked over the specification with a Rootes engineer.

But before I went out on to the road I glanced inside the boot. There came the first big surprise, for there has been a major re-design. It now has $10\frac{3}{4}$ cubic feet of carrying capacity – nearly double what it was before – and this has been achieved in an ingenious fashion. There are now twin

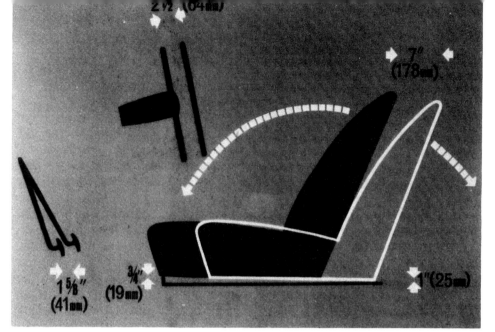

'The number of different driving positions available by simple adjustments to the seats, steering column and pedals verges on the ridiculous.'

fuel tanks, one tucked into each rear wing, holding a total of $11\frac{1}{4}$ gallons, compared with the 9 gallons of the previous model, and connected by a balance pipe. This is a tremendous space saver, and with the spare wheel now sitting vertically at the front end of the boot the result is not only a boot of useful size but one of a very useful shape (helped by dropping the boot floor right down to the level of the sub frame).

There is another advantage in having interconnected twin tanks. It means that though there is only one filler, the fuel automatically feeds into each tank at the same level, and also stays at the same level as it is used up. One large tank on one side of the car could have made an appreciable difference to the car's handling when carrying a full load of fuel.

Car seating, I feel, is quite a problem. The Alpine has solved it with a completely new and fully adjustable seat. This is a lightweight affair, a rally type of seat with foam rubber cushion and foam rubber down the sides of the squab. The base of the seat is on rubber webbing, and I found it not only snug but also extremely comfortable. The base of the seat can be adjusted – it goes up and down three-quarters of an inch at the front and an inch at the rear – so that you can get it at just the angle to suit. There is a very generous range of backwards and forwards movement – no less than eight positions stretching over seven inches.

That isn't all. There is a handle at the side of the seat which enables the squab to be adjusted to any angle – even reclined right back if you feel like a nap.

Behind the seats is useful area which will take small children (or even an adult for a short trip), and for easy access the seats as a whole pivot forwards as well. As no storage space is needed for a hood in the GT model there is even more room.

All this is the sort of thing I like to see in a car, because it means that any driver with any sort of physique or driving habit can be perfectly comfortable.

Another feature I like is the telescopic steering column, which can be adjusted through a range of $2\frac{1}{2}$ inches. The designers have also given thought to another problem – pedal comfort. Have you noticed how often you get into a strange car and comment 'Yes, it's very nice, but the pedals aren't quite right for me?' Well, you can adjust the pedals on the new Alpine. Also the accelerator is now of the organ type. A good idea, this, for a sporting machine, because you can heel-and-toe when making gear changes and so brake at the same time.

Before setting off for a tour of the Warwickshire countryside I had a look under the bonnet. Basically, this is the same 1.6 litre four-cylinder engine that powered the previous model. But there are one or two detail improvements, including larger exhaust valves, which give a slight power increase to 87.75 brake horsepower at 5,200 r.p.m. The stems of both the inlet and exhaust valves are now chromed to give even longer life.

The radiator is different, too. It is now of the vertical flow type, and there is a new fan which gives more efficient cooling. There is also a pipe running from the rear air cleaner to the oil filter which assists the engine breathing.

There was something about the performance for which, at first, I found it difficult to find a reason. The power increase is only quite modest, but the acceleration figures were definitely different. Against the watch the sports tourer produced these figures:

0–30 m.p.h. in 4.5 seconds.
0–50 m.p.h. in 10 seconds.
0–70 m.p.h. in 19.6 seconds.

When I got back to the factory I tackled the engineers about all this. The answer was that while the top gear ratio is still the same (at 3.89 to 1), the indirect ratios have all been increased. This has been done as a result of valuable experience in racing and rallies. Third gear is now 4.8 to 1, second gear 7.381 to 1, and bottom gear 11.538 to 1. A definite improvement, I thought, and in keeping with the car's sporting character. And if you like it as I do – self-cancelling overdrive on third and top gears is available as an extra.

I found the new Alpine a pleasure to drive, but while it is fast it is certainly not 'hairy' – a characteristic that soon makes for fatigue on long journeys.

The car has just the right amount of understeer to satisfy most customers, and the steering is pleasantly positive. The car has the sort of feel which encouraged me to throw it into a corner with plenty of abandon. I knew right away that it could not get me into any trouble.

What has been done is that the cross-member at the front has been reinforced, giving greater rigidity. An anti-roll bar of bigger proportions has been fitted at the front, and the lever-arm piston-type shock absorbers at the rear have been replaced by telescopic dampers. The result is quite impressive.

When I looked under the bonnet I had noticed the servo equipment. Since all the cars I race depend on the disc brakes, I am naturally very sold on the idea. The servo assistance on the Alpine has been adjusted to give just enough help without making the operation seem woolly. I played the brakes hard for a time, and they certainly proved that they can take it.

Most cars have some sort of character (though there are some I could mention which have none at all!). If I had to describe the character of the new Alpine I would say that it is a friendly machine with the ability to eat up the miles in effortless fashion. At the same time it is definitely fun to drive, and if you want to use it hard then it is happy to accept the challenge. Above all it is comfortable, proving that a sporting vehicle need not necessarily land you exhausted at the end of your journey.

All this has been achieved by careful modifications to what was already a sound basic design. Take the electrical system, for example. There is now a headlamp flasher operated from the turn-indicator switch. There are two-speed wipers, a bright-and-dim panel light switch, map light with separate switch, and steady-reading fuel and water temperature gauges – all little things that add up to an improved car. Screen washers, I was glad to learn, are standard equipment.

The designers have gone to great lengths to ensure that the whole car is draught and waterproof, and the quarter lights at the front enable the windows to wind up and down in gutters that very effectively keep out any wet.

I didn't have as much time with the new Alpine as I would have wished, but what I did have the chance to sample convinced me that the Series 3 Alpine is a car that I shall want to drive quite a lot in the future.

Jack Brabham, Twice World Champion, Tests the
SERIES 4 AUTOMATIC ALPINE
Published in 'Modern Motoring and Travel' March 1964
Titled: 'I Drive an Extremely Refined Machine'
In between a couple of disappointing motor races – the South African

'The Alpine has progressed over the years, and there have been a number of minor styling changes in the Series 4 model. The rear wings, for example, have been restyled.' (Mike Green)

Grand Prix, where my car ran into early engine trouble and finally retired with a holed fuel tank, and out in New Zealand, where I had a spectacular high-speed 'incident' with another competitor – I had a few comparatively quiet days in England.

There was in fact plenty of work to do, because I've also decided to build a car to drive at Indianapolis in May, but I just managed to find time for some of the most relaxed motoring I'd had for a long while.

You may find it hard to believe, but when I'm out on public roads I like my driving to be calm, restful and completely lacking in fuss. After all, it makes quite a change from roaring along at well over a hundred miles an hour in a car with an open cockpit and an engine with open exhausts. It also provides an opportunity for catching up on radio programmes!

Well, Rootes found the car to suit me on this occasion, for they sent along their latest Sunbeam Alpine – the Series 4 – and chose one with a think-for-itself gearbox.

In its latest version, the Sunbeam Alpine is really an extremely refined machine. (I remember driving the first of the line around the Avus track in Berlin in 1959, before the German Grand Prix, and feeling that here was a thoroughbred with a very promising future.)

The Alpine has progressed over the years, and there have been a number of minor styling changes in the Series 4 model, though these are comparatively few. The rear wings, for example, have been re-styled, the front grille has been given a more attractive look, and the front and rear lamp clusters are slightly changed.

The overriders, too, now have rubber inserts. This is a splendid device which can prevent a lot of irritating damage in everyday use in crowded streets, especially when parking is tight. Another new feature is the filler

The inside door caping is another distinguishing feature of the G.T. models: it was not included on the Sports Tourers.

cap, which has a very neat flush fitting quick-release mechanism.

When I got into the car – incidentally the Gran Turismo version – I was immediately struck by the tremendous comfort of the seats, which are of foam rubber cushions on rubber webbing. These have a four-position adjustment for height and tilt, and a whole range of fore-and-aft movement over something like seven inches.

The seat squabs can also be angled through several positions all the way back to fully reclining. Since the steering wheel height can quickly be adjusted for height, and the foot controls have two-position adjustments, there's no chance of the Alpine failing to fit any size of driver.

The equipment and finish is of a very high standard. Set in the walnut-veneer facia is a complete range of instruments, and though they

'There's room in the back for small children, and the rear compartment is upholstered for the purpose with plastic foam padding at shoulder height.'

stretch over the facia for quite a distance (because there are so many of them), they are all clearly visible to the driver without effort.

The wood-rimmed steering wheel is a pleasant luxury and provides a sporting touch, and I especially like the generous headroom. There's room in the back for small children like my little boy Gary, and the rear compartment is upholstered for the purpose with plastic-foam padding at shoulder height.

The hinged quarter lights proved very practical in providing a mist-free interior during bad weather, and the trim is of high quality, with tailored carpets to set it all off. I learned that the heater was standard equipment on the GT model, and there are also courtesy lights which operate when the doors are opened.

But by now I've rather come to take good finish and comfortable appointments for granted on Rootes cars. What delighted me even more was the refined performance of this Alpine, with the accent on refinement.

A number of detailed modifications have been made to the 1.6 litre four-cylinder power unit, which, with its aluminium cylinder head, has a maximum output of just under 88 brake horsepower at 5,000 r.p.m. The improvements include a new compound cast-iron exhaust manifold with twin downpipes and a single silencer. The engine is, of course, fitted with the now well-proven Solex twin-choke compound carburettor, which gives smooth running and helps towards fuel economy.

What is more, the engine produces its power with a complete lack of fuss. There must be very few sporty cars which go about their business with less noise. (And so far as the occupants are concerned, the noise level is made even more agreeably low by a generous helping of sound insulation in the body.)

Before I sat in the Alpine I had rather expected to find the automatic gearbox control stick in the usual position on the steering column. Surprise, surprise! The selector stick is in the position normally occupied by the ordinary gearshift on a manual gearbox. It is a neat little selector, operating backwards and forwards, falling easily to hand and quite delightful to operate. All you have to do is to flick it slightly sideways to move it from notch to notch, and the positions are quite clearly marked.

This Borg Warner automatic transmission, the new Type 35, is a revelation. It was designed specifically for cars in the $1\frac{1}{2}$ to 3-litre class, and it does a wonderful job. There are, in fact, three gears, but the changes – both up and down – are so jerk-free that it might almost be an infinitely variable transmission.

Until you've driven the Alpine with this transmission you can have no idea how restful and simple sporty motoring can be. The Borg Warner box does all the thinking for you. I experimented driving off, first in a leisurely fashion with only a whiff of throttle, and trying to spot when the box would change up into the next ratio, and then putting my foot hard down and guessing at what higher speeds this would happen.

Believe me, there's simply nothing to it. Judging by the reaction when Betty, my wife, drove the Alpine, it is definitely going to be a favourite among women motorists, because there's nothing at all to worry about.

And I enjoyed it, too. You are not, however, completely at the mercy of the little man down in the gearbox, because you can keep in a lower gear by selecting "L" for low, and there's also a kick-down on the accelerator.

Naturally you cannot go in for all-out racing with an automatic gearbox car, because it isn't meant for that at all. But I did put in a few very satisfying laps at Brands Hatch (where the European Grand Prix is being held this year), at quite a fair turn of speed, and found it great fun. You can't of course, scream into a corner at high speed and change down into a lower gear, but the lap times weren't at all bad, and they were certainly without drama.

This was due not only to the gearbox but also to the pleasant handling properties of the Alpine. Earlier models always handled well, but further improvements have now been made to the suspension – the springs have been rerated and the dampers improved – giving a smoother ride and even greater cornering power.

And as my laps of Brands convincingly demonstrated, the braking system – with discs on the front wheels and drums at the back – is extremely effective. With vacuum servo assistance pedal pressures are very light – another feature that the ladies will love.

During the short time I had with the new Alpine I learned to appreciate many other features, such as the provision of a headlamp flasher and the two-speed screen wipers.

Here, then, is a car with a useful performance, in which you can cruise smoothly and quietly along a motorway at 80-plus, throw about twisty roads with tremendous confidence, or merely potter along gently without giving the gear lever a thought.

This is the sort of road driving for me. I'm glad Rootes have taken the lead in bringing out the first two-pedal volume-production $1\frac{1}{2}$ litre sports car in Europe. And there are no greasing points to think about, either!

'Autocar' Road Test Number 2079
Published in 'Autocar' – 13th May 1966
Make: SUNBEAM ALPINE SERIES 5 (1724 c.c.)

Test Conditions
Weather: dry and overcast, with 5–10 m.p.h. wind
Barometer: 29.5 H.G.
Temperature: 7° C. (45° F.)
Dry concrete and asphalt surfaces.

Weight
Kerb weight (with oil, water and half full fuel tank):   2,246 lb.
Front – rear distribution, per cent: F–51.6; R–48.4
Laden as tested: 2,582 lb.

Turning Circles
Between kerbs: L–31 ft. 8 ins.;   R–33 ft. 2 ins.
Between walls: L–33 ft. 6 ins.;   R–34 ft. 11 ins.
Steering wheel turns lock to lock: 3.6

Performance Data
Overdrive top gear m.p.h. per 1,000 r.p.m.:   20.3
Top gear m.p.h. per 1,000 r.p.m.:   16.3
Mean piston speed at max power: 2,980 ft./min.
Engine revs. at mean maximum speed (overdrive):   4,825 r.p.m.
B.h.p. per ton laden: 80.0

Fuel: Premium (96.2–98.6 r.m.)
Test distance: 1,317 miles
Overall consumption: 25.5 m.p.g.
Normal range: 23–30 m.p.g.
Oil: S.A.E. 20W
Oil consumption: 220 m.p.p.

Speed Range and Time in Seconds

m.p.h.	o/d top	top	o/d third	third	second	first
10–30	—	—	—	9.0	5.0	3.2
20–40	16.2	11.0	10.7	7.7	4.4	—
30–50	16.6	10.0	9.8	7.0	—	—
40–60	16.6	10.1	9.5	7.4	—	—
50–70	17.1	10.5	11.4	10.3	—	—
60–80	20.7	13.1	16.1	—	—	—
70–90	—	24.3	25.7	—	—	—

Brakes

	pedal load	retardation	equiv. distance
From 30 m.p.h.	25 lb.	0.23 g.	131 ft.
in neutral	50 lb.	0.45 g.	67 ft.
	75 lb.	0.72 g.	42 ft.
	150 lb.	1.00 g.	30.1 ft.
Handbrake		0.35 g.	86 ft.

Fuel Consumption Constant Speed on Level

	m.p.g. overdrive top gear	m.p.g. direct top gear
30 m.p.h.	48.2	44.5
40 m.p.h.	44.5	39.6
50 m.p.h.	39.6	35.7
60 m.p.h.	34.8	31.2
70 m.p.h.	31.7	28.0
80 m.p.h.	27.6	23.4
90 m.p.h.	23.4	19.4

Acceleration Times (in Seconds) from Standstill

0–30	4.4
0–40	6.8
0–50	9.8
0–60	13.6
0–70	18.3
0–80	26.2
0–90	42.9
Standing ¼ mile	19.1 seconds

Sunbeam Alpine Series V

Sports car fashions, equipment and fittings have changed a lot in the past decade. One of the first models to break with the old he-man tradition, by offering wind-up windows, comfortable seating and plenty of space, was the Sunbeam Alpine. Introduced in 1959 with a structure based largely on a Hillman Husky floor, 1,494 c.c. 78 b.h.p. Sunbeam Rapier engine and gearbox, the Alpine has been revised several times in the intervening seven years. The engine became 1,592 c.c. for Series II, reclining seats and a smart GT hardtop model appeared in Series III, while a new hood mechanism, together with the trimming down of tail fins identified Series

IV. The latest revision – to Series V – places more emphasis on mechanical improvements than before. In common with other Rootes models for 1966, the engine has been given a longer-stroke, five main-bearing crankshaft which increases capacity to 1,725 c.c.; however, only the Alpine is fitted with twin constant-vacuum Stromberg 150 CD carburettors. Though the gearbox has included synchromesh on bottom for nearly two years, the latest car has its own special close-ratio set matched to the new engine tune.

Thus equipped, along with the optional overdrive, adjustable steering column and a wide range of instruments, the Series V Alpine is a thoroughly practical sporting car offering nearly saloon car comforts at a very reasonable price. Indeed, since 1959, despite all the mechanical and styling changes, the basic price of this open sports car has increased by only £40, to £725, which is no mean achievement.

In spite of the progressive power increases and a careful control on all-up weight, Alpines are not really much quicker now than ever they were. Unfortunately we cannot make comparisons with our Series IV test car, as this was the heavier GT model with optional automatic transmission (no longer available on Series V). The last open car we tried was a Series II back in 1960, and the last manual car a Series II back in 1963. Acceleration through the gears, and performance in any one gear has been marginally improved, although the real gain of the new close ratio box has been to make the latest car less fussy to drive. Even when using overdrive, and under favourable wind conditions, 100 m.p.h. was barely possible; 90 m.p.h. was none the less a comfortable cruising speed on motorways and could be maintained with little strain.

The Alpine is normally sold without overdrive, and a 3.89 axle ratio, while our test car had the overdrive and 4.22 axle ratio that goes with it. The 3.89 ratio gives gearing at 18.7 m.p.h. per 1,000 r.p.m. in top, and a genuine 100 m.p.h. might be possible without over-revving.

Overdrive

The optional Laycock overdrive is electrically controlled by a self-centring switch, and operates on third and top; it is automatically disengaged when changing out of the top-3rd plane of the gate into bottom or second. Changes can be made direct from O.D. third to O.D. top of course. What is nominally a 6-speed set of gears is spoilt – as often happens – by overdrive third and direct top having almost the same ratio. Acceleration figures in O.D. third were a little better than in direct top up to 70 m.p.h.; above this speed the extra friction in the overdrive made direct top more efficient. O.D. third was good for 94 m.p.h. and top 96 m.p.h.

Compared with the Series III, acceleration through the gears is a little better, more particularly at higher speeds where wind resistance begins to take effect. From 0–60 m.p.h. takes 13.6 sec. (Series III took 14.9), while a standing-start quarter-mile needs 19.1 sec. (19.8 sec). The special close-ratio gearbox has well planned steps; bottom is good for about 30 m.p.h. and second goes on to 47, although this could have been better slightly higher for passing slow-moving traffic on winding roads.

The Alpine engine is only mildly tuned – with 53 b.h.p./litre – and is a very docile unit for slow, town work. Carburation is good and the engine runs evenly at all speeds; however towards the end of the test period the plugs gave trouble and had to be replaced. It pulls strongly without snatch from as low as 1,000 r.p.m., and is still breathing well when the rev counter needle enters the danger zone starting at 6,000 r.p.m. (We limited speeds in all the gears to this figure.) There was quite a lot of induction noise and our road test car produced a painful grating resonance through the throttle linkage, which eventually fell apart.

The Alpine is easy to start from cold, but needs a lot of choke during the first few minutes running. Difficult hot-starting was one of the troubles with the earlier Sunbeam Alpines; we were particularly pleased to find that the Stromberg carburettors seem to have cured this at last.

Fuel Consumption
Most of our staff like driving comfortable sporting cars, and one or two found excuses to rush off on journeys in the Sunbeam. Nearly everyone drove it quickly where traffic conditions allowed, so that the overall fuel consumption figure – 25.5 m.p.g. – is very good. Our constant-speed measurements show that this must be a very carefully developed engine tune; consumption at 30 m.p.h. in overdrive top gear is 48.4 m.p.g. Even at 70 m.p.h. we recorded 31.7 m.p.g. and overdrive always gives an extra 10 m.p.h. cruising speed at no extra fuel cost. Super-premium petrol is not needed, the aluminium cylinder head, with its 9.2 compression ratio, dealing with premium grade without protest. The average Alpine owner, who may not use all the performance all the time, should chalk up to 28 m.p.g. without effort and should manage 300 miles on a tankful of petrol.

The flush-fitting, snap-action, fuel filler cap in the offside rear wing is neat, and accepted full flow from pump nozzles until the twin tanks were nearly full.

Suspension is supple, and reminds one of several continental sports cars rather than its obvious British competitiors. The optional Road Speed tyres help the basically very sound suspension balance to produce really safe, predictable road holding. The steering is low geared, and strongly self-centring; this gives the impression of considerable understeer when entering sharp bends. Twisting roads are best tackled with some verve because the combination of a fairly heavy car and a front-end which tends to plough safely towards the outside of bends makes a normal approach hard work. In fact, the car is well-balanced enough to allow it to be set up in advance and help the tail to come round. On a long bend, the understeer gradually and predictably changes to a more neutral attitude, which is almost automatically corrected by slight wheel movements.

Suspension
That this is after all a fairly firmly sprung sports car becomes apparent when driving over rough ground. On the M.I.R.A. washboard surface the body felt especially rigid at normal speeds, although anything below 20 m.p.h. caused the scuttle and screen to shake around quite appreciably. At 60 m.p.h. there was virtually no vibration at all. Ride on the pavé was good, but the simple rear suspension (by half-elliptic springs and a live axle) has limitations of movement and control; there was appreciable axle-hop, and these movements tended to tweak the rear of the car sideways quite abruptly. Long-wave pitches proved rather unpleasant, as the car bucked up at the rear first, above 50 m.p.h.

All that needs to be said about the brakes is that they are a servo-assisted Girling, mixed disc-drum system. Firm and progressive, with excellent 'feel' and apparently very resistant to fade, they are as safe and predictable as we would expect. Surprisingly high pedal pressures are required from the servo-assisted system for it takes a manly push of 150 lb. to record 1.0 g braking.

Leverage on the pull-up handbrake, mounted snugly between the driver's door and the seat, is almost ideal, but a strong tug is needed to prevent the car from rolling back on a 1-in-3 test hill. Restart was easy and immediate. Use of the handbrake in emergencies would only produce about 0.25 g. The window winding handle has at last been moved so that it is now well clear of the handbrake lever.

Driving Position
Drivers of all shapes and sizes quickly make themselves comfortable in the Alpine, for the driving position is adjustable in several ways. Not only can the seats be moved back and forward as usual (through 6in.) and their deep backrests adjusted for rake through a wide range, but the steering column is adjustable for reach and the pedal cluster can be moved with the aid of a spanner. Steering column adjustment is particularly simple. The boss in the centre of the wheel is turned to release the clamp, and the wheel can then be moved back and forth through 2.5in. and locked in any intermediate position. Padded rolls on the seat cushion and backrest locate

driver and passenger very securely; no effort is needed to hold oneself in place when cornering hard.

With front seats in their normal position, there is really no room for people to sit on the carpeted shelf behind. One adult might just squeeze in – sideways and uncomfortably – for short distances, but children would manage better, as with the hood up headroom is limited. The base of the shelf lifts to reveal the battery, well away from engine and transmission heat.

Stowage Space
This shelf is really intended as extra stowage space for coats and maybe a picnic hamper. There is a small open compartment in front of the passenger (with a map reading lamp above it, and a grab handle in its padded lip), while an oblong, locking box is mounted between the seats as an armrest. Neither is big enough, however, for a camera or lady's handbag.

Road test Alpines usually arrive with a full range of instruments and of these the ammeter and accurate clock are still extras. Blanking plates are easily removed to fit them into the leathercloth covered panel. (On the alternative GT model the facia is polished walnut.) Rootes instruments are always crisply styled and plainly calibrated with white figures on a black ground, and Dayglo red pointers. The fuel gauge is marked in gallons and litres, and the speedometer has a secondary kilometer scale. The all-important oil pressure gauge is immediately in front of the driver, between the speedometer and rev counter, whereas the other minor instruments, controls and switches are scattered around the panel. Sensibly, the wiper switch and washer button are next to each other.

Headlamp mainbeam and indicator warning lights have roll-down lenses special to Rootes which can be adjusted like tiny translucent eyelids to reduce the glare at night. The overdrive tell-tale is no longer fitted.

Pedal layout is excellent. The organ-pedal throttle control enables easy heel and toe changes; when the left foot is not working the clutch it can be rested on the rubber cap of the dipswitch, tight up against the tunnel.

With such a well-planned interior, and luxuries such as the oil cooler and folding hood, we were surprised to find that a heater costs over £18 extra. (It is, however, standard on the GT.) Plenty of really warm air is supplied, but there are no face level vents, and it is impossible to send cool air on to the screen while heating the foot wells. New on the Series V, however, are independent cold air vents which channel ram-air into the footwells at knee height, a refreshing feature for heat waves and hot climates.

Hood

The Alpine has always offered a neat, easily stowed hood, but there have been further refinements in the last couple of years. Stability and good sealing around the door glasses are assured by using rigid members from the screen to the hood pivots behind the seats (these bars fold down for stowage). A rigid bar with four positive fastenings fits snugly against the screen rail, and above the door glasses twin lengths of nylon burr zips bind the fabric to the folding rails and ensure an air-tight fit. When performed in the correct sequence, hood stowage is quick and easy. The hinged steel panels of earlier models have gone, and the hood now disappears into a short, full-width box with built-in tonneau cover which neatly covers the folded fabric, or the hole when the hood is erect.

Door glasses, with fixed quarter lights, and the deep screen, fend off most of the wind when the hood is down, but above about 70 m.p.h. there is quite a lot of turbulence and back draught.

Maintenance is down to a practical minimum. There are no greasing points at all, and oil changes are at 6,000-mile intervals. The dipstick is short and inaccessible, hiding between the distributor and the oil filter, and masked by the coil and a scuttle stiffening tube.

No one seriously expects sports cars to be draughty, noisy and uncomfortable these days. Complete weather protection, comfortable seats and adequate luggage room, with docile road manners and close to 100 m.p.h. are now demanded by the enthusiast. The Alpine Series V provides all these and, although approaching its seventh birthday in July, continual improvements in equipment and power output have maintained its competitive position.

II Identification of Engine and Chassis Numbers

One of the most enlightening aspects of running the Sunbeam Alpine Owners Club was finding out how many people owning Alpines did not know which series car they owned, mainly because the identification badges on the wings and boot had disappeared over the years. Let me now throw a bit of light on the subject. All you have to do is locate the chassis number, which can be found on the chassis identification plate fitted to the bonnet lock platform. If for any reason this plate has become unattached, the engine number is identical to the chassis number and can be located on the engine block just above the petrol pump, providing of course that the engine is the original engine fitted in the car by the manufacturer and not a replacement.

The series of the vehicle can now be identified from these numbers:

Commencing chassis number		*Series of vehicle*
B9000001		Series 1
B9100001		Series 2
B9150001		Series 2 CKD*
B9200001		Series 3
B9250001		Series 3 CKD*
B9400001		Series 4
B9450001		Series 4 CKD*
B941000001	Late	Series 4
B94600001	Late	Series 4 CKD*
B395000001		Series 5
B395900001		Series 5 CKD*

*CKD refers to an Alpine which was sent abroad in 'kit form' for assembling in that country (by authorized dealers). These countries included Italy, South Africa, and Venezuela. It is believed that many were sent to other countries, but owing to the lack of records it is not known just how many were sent or the countries they were sent to.

As with all Rootes vehicles, following these numbers there will be a combination of letters. These fall into two main groups, the first comprising a combination of one to six letters, and the second a combination of three letters, or two letters and one numerical digit.

When two combinations are present on Rootes vehicles, the first indicates:

G.T.   – Gran Turismo (hard top)
B.W.   – Borg Warner automatic transmission
P.O.S. – Power operated steering
O.D.   – Overdrive transmission
E.   – Easidrive automatic transmission
L.   – Low compression engine
M.   – Medium compression engine
H.   – High compression engine

The first letter of the final combination indicates:

H – home market
R – R.H.D. export
L – L.H.D. export
E – CKD export home specification
W – CKD R.H.D. export
X – CKD L.H.D. export

the second letter:
 C – Convertible
 H – Hard top
 R – Roadster
 S – Saloon
 P – Pick-up
 U – Estate car
 V – Van
 X – Chassis only
and the third letter or number:
 M – Ministry of Supply
 O – Standard
 3 – Small bore engine for Bermuda
 X – Non-standard
 P – Police specification

Thus, if your chassis number is: B 941003765 GT. OD/HRO, you own a late type Series 4 Alpine made with a Gran Turismo hard top and overdrive transmission; the vehicle was made for the home market and is a Roadster of standard specification.

III Production Figures

Series	Chassis numbers	Date	Total built
1	B9000001 to B9011904	Oct. 59–Oct. 60	11,904
2	B9100001 to B9119956	Oct. 60–Feb. 63	19,956
3	B9200001 to B9205863	Mar. 63–Jan. 64	5,863
4	B9400001 to B9407936	Jan. 64–Sep. 65	7,936
	B94100001 to B94104470		4,470
5	B395000001 to B395019122	Sep. 65–Jan. 68	19,122
			69,251

Again, due to the lack of documentation, no final production figures are available for the CKD Alpines. The figures shown below are all that are available:

Series	Chassis numbers	Total known kits
2	B9150001 to B9150073	73
3	B9250001 to B9250241	241
4	B9450001 to B9450055	55
		369

IV Performance Figures

Series	B.h.p. gross	B.h.p. nett	Developed at r.p.m.	Max. torque lb./ft.	Developed at r.p.m.
1	83.5	78	5300	89.5	3400/3800
2	85.5	80	5000	94	3800
3 (S.T.D.) Zenith	87.7	82	5200	93	3600
3 (G.T.) Zenith	80.2	75	5000	92	3600
3 (S.T.D.) Solex	86	80.5	5000	93.4	3500
3 (G.T.) Solex	82.5	77	5000	91	3500
4	86.1	80.5	5000	93.4	3500
5	96.8	90.5	5400	103	3700

Road speed in m.p.h. at 1,000 r.p.m. (Note: speeds for North American Alpines are lower.)

Series	Standard Top gear	Overdrive Direct top gear	o/d top gear
1	17.3	15.9	19.8
2	17.3	15.9	19.8
3	17.6	17.6	21.9
4	17.6	16.2	20.2
5	17.82	16.4	22.2
5 (Dunlop R.S.5 tyres)	17.71	16.3	20.3

V Comparison of Performance Figures Obtained in Road Tests

SERIES 1
Basic price inclusive of U.K. tax: £971 10s 10d (Sports)

Extras:				
	overdrive	£60	4s	2d
	wire wheels	£38	5s	0d
	hard top	£60	0s	0d

Magazine	Road & Track	Motor	Autocar	Autosport	Cars Illus.
Date	May 1960	18.11.59	4.9.59	23.10.59	Jan. 1960
Type (G.T. or Sports)	Sports			G.T.	G.T.
Speeds in gears in m.p.h. (best)					
O/D4		100.6	101.0	102.2	103.0
4	95.0	91.0	91.0	94.0	95.0
O/D3		81.0	82.0	86.0	84.0
3	72.0	65.0	66.0	68.0	70.0
O/D2					
2	47.0	42.0	45.0	45.0	45.0
1	30.0	27.0	28.0	30.0	
Acceleration in secs.					
0–30 m.p.h.	4.8	4.9	5.1	4.2	4.5
0–40 m.p.h.	7.0	7.0	7.1		7.0
0–50 m.p.h.	10.6	10.2	10.6	9.0	9.8
0–60 m.p.h.	15.2	13.6	14.0	13.7	13.8
0–70 m.p.h.	21.8	17.9	18.4		21.0
0–80 m.p.h.	30.0	24.7	27.5	25.6	
Standing ¼ mile	20.6	19.7	19.8	19.0	
Fuel consumption in m.p.g. (constant speed on level, O/D top gear)					
@ 30 m.p.h.		46.0	54.0		
@ 40 m.p.h.		45.0	50.0		
@ 50 m.p.h.		39.5	42.5		
@ 60 m.p.h.		35.0	36.0		
@ 70 m.p.h.		31.0	31.0		
Overall fuel consumption in m.p.g.	22–26	27.4	25.5		

SERIES 2
Basic price inclusive of U.K. tax: £985 14s 2d (Sports)
Extras: overdrive   £60   4s 2d
                  wire wheels   £38   5s 0d
                  hardtop

Magazine	*Motor*	*Road & Track*	*Autocar*	*Track & Traffic*	*Cars Illus.*
Date	28.12.60	Oct. 1961	2.12.60	May 1961	May 1961
Type (G.T. or Sports)	G.T.			G.T.	Sports
Speeds in gears in m.p.h. (best)					
O/D4	101.1		98.0		
4	91.0	100.0	94.0	96.2	100.0
O/D3	81.0		87.0		
3	65.0	60.0	68.0		80.0
O/D2					
2	42.0	42.0	44.0		50.0
1	27.0	25.0	28.0		
Acceleration in secs.					
0–30 m.p.h.	4.3	5.6	4.5	4.5	5.0
0–40 m.p.h.	6.4	8.4	6.6	6.6	6.5
0–50 m.p.h.	9.9	12.8	10.3	10.0	8.2
0–60 m.p.h.	13.6	18.1	14.8	14.0	13.0
0–70 m.p.h.	19.0	27.0	20.3	19.3	16.2
0–80 m.p.h.	26.0	37.6	29.8	27.2	22.0
Standing $\frac{1}{4}$ mile	19.4	21.2	19.7		
Fuel consumption in m.p.g. (constant speed on level, O/D top gear)					
@ 30 m.p.h.	48.0		51.3		
@ 40 m.p.h.	45.5		46.1		
@ 50 m.p.h.	40.0		40.0		
@ 60 m.p.h.	34.5		34.5		
@ 70 m.p.h.	30.5		29.8		
Overall fuel consumption	26.0	19/25	20.6	27.0	25.0

SERIES 3

Basic price inclusive of U.K. tax: £840　7s　1d (Sports)
　　　　　　　　　　　　　　　£899　11s　3d (G.T.)

Extras:	overdrive	£51　7s　1d
	wire wheels	£32　12s　6d

Magazine	Car & Driver	Motor	Cars Illus.	Autocar	Road & Track
Date	Oct. 1963	25.9.63	May 1963	20.9.63	
Type (G.T. or Sports)	G.T.	Sport	G.T.	G.T.	G.T.
Speeds in gears in m.p.h. (best)					
O/D4		97.0	97.0	95.0	100.0
4	96.5		92.0	98.0	
O/D3			91.0	95.0	
3	77.2	82.2	78.0	79.0	77.0
O/D2					
2	51.0	51.4	58.0	51.0	50.0
1	32.5	35.0		33.0	32.0
Acceleration in secs.					
0–30 m.p.h.	5.1	4.6	4.0	4.5	5.4
0–40 m.p.h.	8.4	7.4	7.0	7.0	8.6
0–50 m.p.h.	11.8	10.0	10.5	10.1	12.0
0–60 m.p.h.	16.6	14.4	15.5	14.9	18.1
0–70 m.p.h.	21.6	20.4	21.6	20.8	25.0
0–80 m.p.h.	30.8	28.2	33.0	33.0	36.9
Standing ¼ mile	21.3	19.9		19.8	22.2
Fuel consumption in m.p.g. (constant speed on level, O/D top gear)					
@ 30 m.p.h.				59.0	
@ 40 m.p.h.				55.5	
@ 50 m.p.h.				45.0	
@ 60 m.p.h.				37.5	
@ 70 m.p.h.				30.0	
Overall fuel consumption				24.9	20–27

SERIES 4
Basic price inclusive of U.K. tax: £852   8s 9d (Sports)
                                    £912 17s 1d (G.T.)
Extras: overdrive   £51   7s 1d
                wire wheels   £37 15s 6d
                Borg Warner
                auto. gearbox   £90 12s 6d

Magazine	*Motor*	*Autocar*	*Cars Illus.*	*Road & Track*
Date	10.10.64	22.5.64	March, 1964	
Type (G.T. or Sports)	G.T. (auto)	G.T. (auto)	G.T.	G.T. (auto)
Speeds in gears in m.p.h. (best)				
O/D4	92.2 (top)	92.0 (top)	94.6	90.0 (top)
4	61.0 (inter)	64.0 (inter)	93.0	64.0 (inter)
O/D3	41.0 (low)	42.0 (low)	83.0	38.0 (low)
3			64.0	
O/D2				
2			42.0	
1			29.0	
Acceleration in secs.				
0–30 m.p.h.	6.8	7.0	4.4	6.2
0–40 m.p.h.	9.2	9.7	6.1	8.9
0–50 m.p.h.	13.0	13.3	10.2	12.3
0–60 m.p.h.	18.0	18.8	13.8	16.5
0–70 m.p.h.	27.2	25.6	19.6	26.0
0–80 m.p.h.	39.0	39.7	30.6	35.0
Standing ¼ mile	21.8	22.5	19.2	21.0
Overall fuel consumption	24.3	20.9	22–25	18–22

SERIES 5

Basic price inclusive of U.K. tax: £877 12s 1d (Sports)
                                    £938   0s 0d (G.T.)
Extras: overdrive   £51   7s 1d
               wire wheels

Magazine	Autocar	Sporting Motorist	Car & Car Conversions	Motor Sport
Date	13.5.66	Feb. 1966	Jan. 1966	Jan. 1966
Type (G.T. or Sports)	Sport	G.T.	Sport	G.T.
Speeds in gears in m.p.h. (best)				
O/D4	100.0	100.0		
4	96.0	98.0	97.0	
O/D3	94.0	95.0		
3	73.0	78.0	78.0	74.0
O/D2				
2	47.0	48.0	48.0	50.0
1	30.0	30.0	30.0	31.0
Acceleration in secs.				
0–30 m.p.h.	4.4	3.9	3.2	
0–40 m.p.h.	6.8	6.4	5.4	5.9
0–50 m.p.h.	9.8	8.6	7.8	8.8
0–60 m.p.h.	13.6	12.9	11.3	12.9
0–70 m.p.h.	18.3	18.1	15.4	18.2
0–80 m.p.h.	26.2	24.4	21.2	27.0
Standing $\frac{1}{4}$ mile	19.1			19.0
Fuel consumption in m.p.g. (constant speed on level, O/D top gear)				
@ 30 m.p.h.	48.2			
@ 40 m.p.h.	44.5			
@ 50 m.p.h.	39.6			
@ 60 m.p.h.	34.8			
@ 70 m.p.h.	31.7			
Overall fuel consumption	25.5	24.4	20.0	24.0

VARIOUS

			Conversion		
Basic price inc. of U.K. tax:	£1494 15s 7d	£1225	£24 15s 0d without fitting		

Magazine	Autocar	Autosport	Autocar	Motor	Car & Driver
Date	16.2.62	21.4.61	5.7.63	27.12.61	April 1962
Type	Harrington Le Mans	Harrington Stage 3	Series 2 + Nerus convers.	Harrington Le Mans	Harrington Le Mans
Speed in gears in m.p.h. (best)					
O/D4	105.8	111.6	104.5	109.1	108.0
4	92.0	98.0	95.0	89.0	100.0
O/D3	81.0	90.0	87.0	80.0	
3	65.0	72.0	68.0	64.0	75.0
O/D2	52.0				
2	42.0	50.0	44.0	42.0	48.0
1	28.0	32.0	28.0	27.0	32.0
Acceleration in secs.					
0–30 m.p.h.	4.5	3.9	4.8	4.2	4.3
0–40 m.p.h.	6.5	5.8	6.8	6.5	6.7
0–50 m.p.h.	9.0	7.8	9.7	10.0	10.2
0–60 m.p.h.	13.0	10.6	12.3	13.3	14.4
0–70 m.p.h.	17.6	15.6	16.2	17.0	19.6
0–80 m.p.h.	24.8	21.2	21.6	23.0	27.4
Standing ¼ mile	19.3	17.9	18.9	19.2	20.0
Fuel consumption in m.p.g. (constant speed on level, O/D top gear)					
@ 30 m.p.h.	45.0			48.5	
@ 40 m.p.h.	49.0			47.5	
@ 50 m.p.h.	45.0			41.0	
@ 60 m.p.h.	37.0			36.0	
@ 70 m.p.h.	32.0			33.0	
Overall fuel consumption	20.5	22.0	23.9	23.2	18/22

VI Body Dimensions, Weights and Capacities

Body Dimensions	Series 1		Series 2	
	Ft.	In.	Ft.	In.
A. Wheelbase	7	2	as Series 1	
B. Front overhang	2	$3\frac{3}{4}$	,,	,,
C. Rear overhang	3	$5\frac{1}{2}$	,,	,,
D. Overall length	12	$11\frac{1}{4}$	,,	,,
E. Overall width	5	$0\frac{1}{2}$	,,	,,
F. Overall height	4	$3\frac{1}{2}$	,,	,,
G. Ground clearance		$5\frac{1}{8}$	,,	,,
H. Front clearance angle		$25°$	,,	,,
J. Rear clearance angle		$20°$	,,	,,
K. Windscreen depth	1	4	,,	,,
L. Steering wheel to front squab (min.)		10	1	0
(max.)	1	5	1	7
M. Pedals to seat cushion (min.)	1	2	1	$3\frac{1}{2}$
(max.)	1	9	2	0
N. Rear seat depth	1	$4\frac{1}{2}$	as Series 1	
O. Front headroom	3	0	,,	,,
P. Windscreen width (projected)	3	11	,,	,,
Q. Front seat depth	1	$7\frac{3}{4}$	,,	,,
R. Front seat width	1	$7\frac{1}{2}$	,,	,,
S. Maximum interior width	3	11	,,	,,
T. Rear seat width	3	$2\frac{1}{2}$	,,	,,

The above measurements are approximate and apply to both hard top and soft top.

Plan of body dimensions for Series 1 and 2.

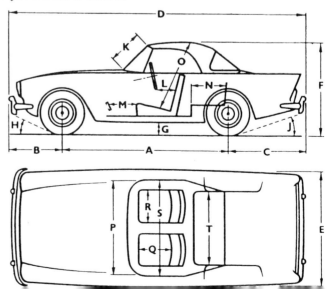

Kerb Weight

Soft top without overdrive	2184 lb.	as Series 1
Soft top with overdrive	2204 lb.	,, ,,
Hard top without overdrive	2218 lb.	,, ,,
Hard top with overdrive	2238 lb.	,, ,,

Capacities

Engine including filter	8 pts.	as Series 1
Gearbox without overdrive	$2\frac{3}{4}$ pts.	,, ,,
Gearbox with overdrive	4 pts.	,, ,,
Rear axle	$1\frac{3}{4}$ pts.	,, ,,
Coolant with heater	15 pts.	,, ,,
Fuel	9 galls.	,, ,,

	Series 3			
	Sports Tourer		Gran Turismo	
Body Dimensions	Ft.	Ins.	Ft.	Ins.
A. Overall length	12	$11\frac{1}{4}$	as S.T.	
B. Front overhang	2	$3\frac{3}{4}$	,,	,,
C. Wheelbase	7	2	,,	,,
D. Rear overhang	3	$5\frac{1}{2}$	,,	,,
E. Overall height	4	$3\frac{1}{2}$	4	$4\frac{1}{2}$
F. Steering wheel to front squab (min.)		$11\frac{1}{2}$	as S.T.	
(max.)	1	$8\frac{3}{4}$	,,	,,
G. Windscreen depth	1	4	,,	,,
H. Front headroom	3	$1\frac{1}{2}$	,,	,,
J. Pedals to seat cushions (min.)	1	$4\frac{3}{4}$	,,	,,
(max.)	2	$1\frac{1}{4}$	,,	,,
K. Rear seat depth	1	$4\frac{1}{2}$	,,	,,
L. Ground clearance (laden)		$4\frac{1}{4}$	,,	,,

Plan of body dimensions for Series 3, 4 and 5.

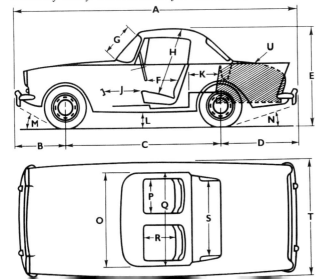

Body dimensions	Ft.	Ins.	Ft.	Ins.
M. Front clearance angle		25°	,,	,,
N. Rear clearance angle		20°	,,	,,
O. Windscreen width (projected)	4	1	,,	,,
P. Front seat width	1	7	,,	,,
Q. Front elbow room	4	3½	,,	,,
R. Front seat depth	1	6	,,	,,
S. Rear seat width	3	1¾	2	11½
T. Overall width	5	0½	as S.T.	
U. Luggage capacity	10¾ cu. ft.		,,	,,

All dimensions are approximate only, and are taken with the vehicle in an unladen condition.

Kerb Weight

Without overdrive	2223 lb.	2278 lb.
With overdrive	2243 lb.	2298 lb.

Capacities

Engine including filter	8 pts.	as S.T.
Gearbox without overdrive	2¾ pts.	,, ,,
Gearbox with overdrive	4 pts.	,, ,,
Rear axle	1¾ pts.	,, ,,
Coolant with heater	12½ pts.	,, ,,
Fuel	11¼ galls.	,, ,,

		Sports Tourer		Gran Turismo	
Body dimensions		Ft.	Ins.	Ft.	Ins.
A. Overall length		13	0	as S.T.	
B. Front overhang		2	3¾	,,	,,
C. Wheelbase		7	2	,,	,,
D. Rear overhang		3	6¼	,,	,,
E. Overall height		4	3½	4	4½
F. Steering wheel to front squab	(min.)		11½	as S.T.	
	(max.)	1	8¾	,,	,,
G. Windscreen depth		1	4	,,	,,
H. Front headroom		3	1½	,,	,,
J. Pedals to seat cushion	(min.)	1	4¾	,,	,,
	(max.)	2	1¼	,,	,,
K. Rear seat depth		1	4½	,,	,,
L. Ground clearance (laden)			4¼	,,	,,
M. Front clearance angle			25°	,,	,,
N. Rear clearance angle			20°	,,	,,

O. Windscreen width (projected)	4	1	,, ,,	
P. Front seat width	1	7	,, ,,	
Q. Front elbow room	4	$3\frac{1}{2}$	,, ,,	
R. Front seat depth	1	6	,, ,,	
S. Rear seat width	3	$1\frac{3}{4}$	2	$11\frac{1}{2}$
T. Overall width	5	$0\frac{1}{2}$	as S.T.	
U. Luggage capacity	$10\frac{3}{4}$ cu. ft.		,, ,,	

All dimensions are approximate only, and are taken with the vehicle in an unladen condition.

Kerb Weight

Without overdrive	2180 lb.	2230 lb.
With overdrive	2200 lb.	2250 lb.

Capacities

Engine including filter	8 pts.	as S.T.
Gearbox without overdrive	$2\frac{3}{4}$ pts.*	,, ,,
Gearbox with overdrive	4 pts.**	,, ,,
Rear axle	$1\frac{3}{4}$ pts.	,, ,,
Coolant with heater	$12\frac{1}{2}$ pts.	,, ,,
Fuel	$11\frac{1}{4}$ pts.	,, ,,

*$3\frac{1}{2}$ pts. from chassis no. B94100000.
**$4\frac{1}{2}$ pts. from chassis no. B94100000.

VII Technical Specifications

General Data

Engine	Series 1	Series 2	Series 3	Series 4	Series 5
Capacity	1494 cc	1592 cc	1592 cc	1592 cc	1724 cc
Number of cylinders	4	4	4	4	4
Bore	3.11 in.	3.21 in.	3.21 in.	3.21 in.	3.21 in.
Stroke	3 in.	3 in.	3 in.	3 in.	3.25 in.
Compression ratio	9.2:1	9.1:1	9.1:1	9.2:1	9.2:1
Maximum b.h.p. (net)	78	80	82	80.5	92.5
@ r.p.m.	5,300	5,000	5,200	5,000	5,500
Maximum torque lb/ft.	89.5	94	93	93	103
@ r.p.m.	3,400	3,800	3,600	3,500	3,700
Oil pressure (hot) at					
50 m.p.h. lbs./sq. in.	30/50	30/50	40/50	55/65	40

Ignition					
Static timing (full retard)					
all b.t.d.c.	5–7	5–7	9–11	9–11	6–10
Sparking plug type (Champion)	N5	N5	N5	N9Y	N9Y
Sparking plug gap	.025 in.	.025 in.	.025 in.	.025 in.	.025 in.
Distributor contact gap	.016 in.	.016 in.	.015 in.	.015 in.	.015 in.

Valves						
Rocker clearance (hot)	inlet	.012 in.	.012 in.	.012 in.	.012 in.	.012 in.
	exhaust	.014 in.	.014 in.	.014 in.	.014 in.	.014 in.
Timing	inlet opens	14 b.t.d.c	14 b.t.d.c	14 b.t.d.c	*19 b.t.d.c	29 b.t.d.c
	inlet closes	52 a.b.d.c	52 a.b.d.c	52 a.b.d.c	*57 a.b.d.c	63 a.b.d.c
	exhaust opens	56 b.b.d.c.	56 b.b.d.c.	56 b.b.d.c	*61 b.b.d.c	69 b.b.d.c.
	exhaust closes	10 a.t.d.c.	10 a.t.d.c.	10 a.t.d.c.	*15 a.t.d.c.	23 a.t.d.c.

*From chassis number B.94100000: All Series 4 vehicles prior to this as per Series 3 timings.

Cylinder Block

Material	cast iron
Max. oversize with or without liners	0.040
Linering size Series 1	3.254 in./3.255 in.
Linering size Series 2, 3, 4	3.354 in./3.355 in.
Linering size Series 5	3.357 in./3.358 in.
Interference fit	0.002 in./0.004 in.

Cylinder Head

Material	aluminium
Size of cylinder head studs	$\frac{3}{8}$ in. U.N.F.
Gasket – type	steel/copper/asbestos
Thickness	0.030 in. compressed
Compression pressure Series 1	170/180 lb./in.^{2}
Compression pressure Series 2, 3, 4	185/195 lb./in.^{2}
Compression pressure Series 5	175/185 lb./in.^{2}

Valves

Position and operation	overhead, push rods and rockers
Head diameter – inlet	1.436 in./1.432 in.
From B9117425 – inlet	1.475 in./1.471 in.
Series 5 – inlet	1.505 in./1.501 in.
exhaust	1.176 in./1.172 in.
Series 5 – exhaust	1.206 in./1.202 in.
Angle of seat in cylinder head inlet and exhaust	45°
Angle of valve face	45°
Valve stem diameter – inlet	0.3110 in./0.3105 in.
exhaust	0.3100 in./0.3095 in.
Valve stem clearance in guide – inlet	0.0010 in./0.0025 in.
exhaust	0.0020 in./0.0035 in.
Series 5 – inlet	0.0015 in./0.0030 in.
exhaust	0.0025 in./0.0040 in.
Length of valves	4.66 in.
Valve spring – type	dual
– retention	cup and split cottors
– fitted length inner	1.43 in.
– fitted length outer	1.55 in.
– free length inner	1.93 in.
– free length outer	2.23 in.
– load fitted inner	35.9 lb.
– load fitted outer	70.8 lb.

Valve guides – outside diameter   0.5640 in./0.5635 in.
       – length inlet   2.0 in.
       – length exhaust   2.15˙in.
       – interference fit   0.0025 in./0.0045 in.
       – fitted height above head 0.50 in.

Camshaft

No. of bearings	3
Type of bearings	steel back white metal
End thrust	location plate at front
Drive	duplex chain
Lubrication	oil jet
Chain tensioner	spring blade
End float	0.002 in./0.004 in.
Journal diameters	1.7477 in./1.7470 in.

Crankshaft

Balance: integrally forged counterweights.

Number of main bearings – Series, 1, 2, 3, 4	3
Series 5,	5
Type of main bearings	steel shell white metal
Diameter of main journals Series 1, 2, 3, 4	2.365 in./2.375 in.
Series 5	2.249 in./2.2495 in.
Diameter of crankpin bearings Series 1	1.8755 in./1.876 in.
Series 2, 3, 4	2.0005 in./2.001 in.
Series 5	2.115 in./2.125 in.
End float Series 1, 2, 3, 4	0.002 in./0.004 in.
Series 5	0.002 in./0.008 in.
Main bearing running clearance	0.0010 in./0.0025 in.
Maximum undersize for regrinding	
Series 1, 2, 3, 4	0.06 in.
Series 5	0.04 in.

Connecting Rod

Material	steel forging
Type	'H' section
Distance between centres Series 1, 2, 3, 4	5.751 in./5.749 in.
Series 5	5.626 in./5.624 in.
Big end bearings	steel shell with copper–lead bearing, indium coated

15

Appendices

Big end bore (without bearings) Series 1   2.0215 in./2.0210 in.
                             Series 2, 3, 4   2.1465 in/2.1460 in.
                             Series 5   2.2715 in./2.2710 in.

Big end bearing running clearance   0.0015 in./0.002 in.
Big end, end float   0.0125 in./0.0075 in.
Small end bore size (bushed) Series 1

high grade	0.8753 in./0.8752 in.	(painted white)
medium grade	0.8752 in./0.8751 in.	(painted green)
low grade	0.8751 in./0.8750 in.	(painted yellow)
	Series 2, 3, 4, 5	
high grade	0.9379 in./0.9378 in.	(painted white)
medium grade	0.9378 in./0.9377 in.	(painted green)
low grade	0.9377 in./0.9376 in.	(painted yellow)

Gudgeon Pin

Type   floating
Location   circlips
Diameter: Series 1

high grade	0.8752 in./0.8751 in.	(painted white)
medium grade	0.8751 in./0.8750 in.	(painted green)
low grade	0.8750 in./0.8749 in.	(painted yellow)
	Series 2, 3, 4, 5	
high grade	0.9377 in./0.9376 in.	(painted white)
medium grade	0.9376 in./0.9375 in.	(painted green)
low grade	0.9375 in./0.9374 in.	(painted yellow)

Pistons

Type   slotted
Material   aluminium alloy tin plated
Length   3.25 in.
Rings – compression   two
         – scraper   one
Compression – identific mark on crown   H.C. (high)
     L.C. (low)

Pistol bowl volume   H.C. 6.9–7.5 c.c.
     L.C. 15.3–15.7 c.c.

Max. permissible weight variation per set   2 drams.
Diameter of piston   Series 1
   grade A   3.1088 in./3.1092 in.
   grade B   3.1092 in./3.1096 in.
   grade C   3.1096 in./3.1100 in.
   grade D   3.1100 in./3.1104 in.

	Series 2, 3
grade A	3.2088 in./3.2092 in.
grade B	3.2092 in./3.2096 in.
grade C	3.2096 in./3.2100 in.
grade D	3.2100 in./3.2104 in.
	Series 4, 5
grade A	3.2092 in./3.2096 in.
grade B	3.2096 in./3.2100 in.
grade C	3.2100 in./3.2104 in.
grade D	3.2104 in./3.2108 in.

Piston ring clearance (between ring and groove)	0.0015 in./0.0035 in.
Ring gap top ring Series 1	0.012 in./0.020 in.
Series 2, 3, 4, 5	0.024 in./0.032 in.
second and third ring	0.009 in./0.014 in.

Carburation

Series 1 with gauze type air filter

Make	2 × Zenith
Type	36 W.I.P. 2
Choke	28 m.m.
Main discharge jet	016289
Main jet	130
By-pass jet	blank
High speed bleed	100
Slow running	50
Progression holes	2 × 0.8
Pump jet	50

Series 2 with gauze type air filter

Make	2 × Zenith	2 × Zenith
Type	36 W.I.P. 2	36 W.I.P. 3
Choke	30 m.m.	30 m.m.
Main discharge jet	016289	016289
Main jet	142	142
By-pass jet	blank	blank
High speed bleed	100	100
Slow running	50	45
Progression holes	2 × 0.8	2 × 1.0
Pump jet	*50	70

N.B. Export car settings may differ.

*70 accelerator pump jet is used if 7 m.m. radius pump cam is fitted. Where this cam and jet are used, there is a 50 leak hole in the accelerator pump suction valve.

Series 2 with dry element type air filter

Make	2 × Zenith	2 × Zenith
Type	36 W.I.P. 2	36 W.I.P. 3
Choke	28 m.m.	28 m.m.
Main discharge jet	016219	016219
Main jet	112	112
By-pass jet	57	57
High speed bleed	60	60
Slow running	45	45
Progression holes	2 × 0.8	1 × 1.1 + 1 × 1.0
Pump jet	70	70

Series 3	*(S.T.D.)*	*(G.T.)*
	with gauze type air filter	*with dry element type air filter*
Make	2 × Zenith	2 × Zenith
Type	36 W.I.P. 3	36 W.I.P. 3
Choke	29 m.m.	29 m.m.
Main discharge jet	016289SE	0.16289
Main jet	127	105
By-pass jet	blank	55
High speed jet	100	120
Slow running	45	45
Progression holes	1 × 1.0 2 × 1.1	1 × 0.8 1 × 1.1
Pump jet	90	90

Series 3 and 4		*Series 3 (S.T.D.)*	*Series 3 (G.T.)*	*Series 4 (S.T.D. + G.T.)*
Make		All fitted with Solex Compound (twin choke)		
Type		All fitted with 32 P.A.I.A.		
Choke	*(1)	24 m.m.	24 m.m.	24 m.m.
	*(2)	26 m.m.	26 m.m.	26 m.m.
Main jet	*(1)	120	117.5	120
	*(2)	155	130	155
Air correction	*(1)	210	190	210
	*(2)	210	190	210
Pilot jet	*(1)	60	60	60
	*(2)	60	60	60
Pilot air bleed	*(1)	nil	1.0	1.0
	*(2)	1.0	0.8	1.0
Pump jet	*(1)	70	70	70
	*(2)	nil	nil	nil

*(1) Primary throttle; *(2) Secondary throttle.

Series 5
Make	2 × Stromberg
Type	150 C.D.
Needle type	5 M
Spring	plain (uncoloured) 0.032 in.
Fast idle gap	0.029

Lubrication System

Type of pump	eccentric lobe type
Type of intake	gauze filter on pump
Pump drive	skew gear on camshaft
Normal pressure	(hot at 50 m.p.h.)
Series 1, 2, 3, 4	55 lb./sq. in.
Series 5	40/45 lb./sq. in.
Filter type	full flow

Fuel Pump

Make	A.C.
Operation	lever by eccentric on camshaft
Pressure	$1\frac{1}{2}$–$2\frac{1}{2}$ lb./sq. in.

Cooling System

Type system	centrifugal pump and fan
Pump drive	'V' belt from crankshaft pulley
Thermostat (wax type) opens at	180°F (82°C)
Relief valve pressure (in filler cap)	
Series 1, 2	7 lb./sq. in.
Series 3, 4, 5	9 lb./sq. in.

Ignition System

Type	coil and distributor
Firing order	1 : 3 : 4 : 2
Ignition control	full automatic – vacuum and centrifugal
Distributor – makers, type	Lucas DM2.P.4 or 25 D.4
Makers dispatch no.	
Series 1	40683B
Series 2	40766A or 40799
Series 3	40924B
Series 4	40924A
Series 5	41077
Drive	skewgear on camshaft and offset coupling
Direction of drive	anti-clockwise (viewed from above)

Cam dwell angle	$60° \pm 3°$
Coil make and type	
Series 1, 2	Lucas L.A. 45053E
Series 3, 4, 5	Lucas H.A. 45102

Clutch

Make	Borg and Beck
Type Series 1, 2, 3, 4	single dry plate
Series 5	diaphragm
Operation Series 1, 5	hydraulic
Series 2, 3, 4	hydrostatic
Thrust bearing	carbon ring
Driven plate – diameter Series 1, 2, 3, 4	8 ins.
Series 5	$7\frac{1}{2}$ ins.

Gearbox Ratios

	Series 1	*Series 2*	*Series 3*	*Series 4*	*Series 5*
Overdrive	0.803:1	0.803:1	0.803:1	0.803:1	0.803:1
Top	1.00:1	1.00:1	1.00:1	1.00:1	1.00:1
Third	1.39:1	1.39:1	1.23:1	1.39:1	1.295:1
Second	2.14:1	2.14:1	1.89:1	2.14:1	1.99:1
First	3.35:1	3.35:1	2.96:1	3.35:1	3.12:1
Reverse	4.24:1	4.24:1	3.75:1	4.24:1	3.32:1

Final Drive Ratios

With overdrive	*Series 1*	*Series 2*	*Series 3*	*Series 4*	*Series 5*
Overdrive top	3.39:1	3.39:1	3.12:1	3.39:1	3.388:1
Direct top	4.22:1	4.22:1	3.89:1	4.22:1	4.22:1
Overdrive third	4.72:1	4.72:1	3.85:1	4.72:1	4.388:1
Direct third	5.88:1	5.88:1	4.80:1	5.87:1	5.465:1
Direct second	9.04:1	9.04:1	7.38:1	9.04:1	8.397:1
Direct first	14.13:1	14.13:1	11.53:1	14.13:1	13.166:1
Reverse	17.90:1	17.90:1	14.61:1	17.90:1	14.010:1
Without overdrive					
Top	3.89:1	3.89:1	3.89:1	3.89:1	3.89:1
Third	5.41:1	5.41:1	4.80:1	5.41:1	5.037:1
Second	8.33:1	8.33:1	7.38:1	8.32:1	7.741:1
First	13.01:1	13.01:1	11.53:1	13.01:1	12.137:1
Reverse	16.49:1	16.49:1	14.61:1	16.48:1	13.014:1

Propeller Shaft

Type		open shaft (reverse spline)
Length between centres	Series 1, 2, 3, 4	S.T.D. – 32.25 ins.
	Series 1, 2, 3, 4, 5	O/D – 29.5 ins.
	Series 5	S.T.D. – 32.35 ins.

Rear Axle

Type	semi-floating hypoid
Bearings	bevel pinion – taper roller
Differential & crown wheel assembly	taper roller
Hub	ball
Adjustment	bevel pinion – shims
	differential assembly – shims
Crown wheel to pinion (backlash)	0.005 ins./0.009 ins.
Number of teeth – crown wheel	(3.89) 35
pinion	(3.89) 9
crown wheel	(4.22) 38
pinion	(4.22) 9

Front Suspension

Spring – outside diameter	
Series 1, 2	3.87 ins.
Series 3	4.40 ins.
Series 4, 5	4.47 ins.

Free Length

Up to chassis no. B9106289 and Series 3	11.175 ins.
From B9106290	11.65 ins.
Series 4, 5	12.62 ins.
Castor angle	$3° 50'$
Wheel camber angle	$0° 30' \pm 15'$
Steering axis inclination	$5° 15' \pm 15'$
Toe in	$\frac{1}{8}$ in.
Ackerman angles inner wheel	$22° 45' \pm \frac{1}{2}°$
Ackerman angles outer wheel	$20°$
Front hub and float	0.002 in./0.007 in.

Rear Suspension

Type	semi elliptic
Number of blades Series 1	8
(up to B9203547) Series 2, 3	6

(from B9203548) Series 3, 4   5
             Series 5   6
Laden camber load (to be evenly distri-
  buted over centre line of rear axle)   165 lb.

Steering

Make	Burman 'F'
Type	re-circulating ball
Adjustment – rocker arm	shims

Brakes

Make	Girling
Type	hydraulic
Brake discs material	cast iron
Diameter Series 1, 2	9.5 ins.
Series 3, 4	9.85 ins.
Series 5	10.3 ins.
Linings Series 1, 2	DON 55
Series 3, 4, 5	M40
Brake drums material	cast iron
diameter	9 ins.
linings	DON 24

Torque Loading Figures

Engine	lb./ft.
Cylinder head (tighten when cold)	48
Crankshaft (mains)	55
Con. rod (big-end) Series 1	20
Series 2 onwards	24
Flywheel	40

Gearbox	
Mainshaft nuts	80

Rear axle	
Hypoid bevel pinion nut	110
Axle shaft	180
Crown wheel setscrews	50
Differential bearing cap nuts	53

Propeller shaft	
Universal joint – metal to rubber (where fitted)	50

Front suspension

Fulcrum pin to crossmember mounting bolts (upper)	48
Fulcrum pin to crossmember mounting bolts (lower)	32
Eye bolt – trunnion to link	$\begin{cases} 40 \\ 85 \end{cases}$
Ball pin – stub carrier to link	52
Ball pin – housing to link	33
Shock absorber to spring pan	6
Crossmember to frame	62
Road wheel nut	48
Top swivel bearing to axle carrier Serial 5	44
Bottom swivel bearing to axle carrier Series 5	60
Bottom swivel bearing to bottom link Series 5 $\frac{3}{8}$ in. U.N.F.	26
$\frac{1}{2}$ in. U.N.F.	75

Rear suspension

Rear spring 'U' bolts – Alpine	42

Steering

Box to frame	30
Relay level to frame	30
Steering crosstube ball pin – centre	30
– outer	28
Swing lever to rocker shaft	75

Brakes

Brake disc to hub	38
Caliper to adaptor	52
Steering arm to carrier and adaptor	$\begin{cases} 38 \\ 60 \end{cases}$
Adaptor to carrier	38
Bleed screws	6
Union nuts (male)	7
Union nuts (female)	9
Backplate to casing	17
Wheel cylinder to backplate	12
Steering arm to backplate Series 5	48
Backplate to hub Series 5	34

Alternator (Series 5)

Assembly torque load – brush box screws	10
– diode heat sink fixings	25
– 'through' bolts	45

Index

Abbey Panel and Sheet Metal Co. Ltd., 25
Alexander Engineering, 155
Anstie Airfield, 36, 38
Armstrong, Douglas, 64–6
Armstrong, Siddeley, Parkside Works, 26, 39
Armstrong Whitworth, 39
Ashworth, Jim, 107
Automotive Products, 157, 165
Avis, Les, 54
axles: pitfalls when buying, 176–7; technical specification, 250; tuning kits, 143–4, 159

Ballisat, Keith, 132
Barrette, Filippo, 118–25
Bateman, Brian, 29
Beck, Ernie, 107
Bodywork, 172–5
Borg-Warner, 65
Bourke, Bob, 20
Brabham, Jack, 114–16, 213–21
brakes: pitfalls when buying, 176; technical specification, 251; tuning kits, 157
Bristol Siddeley Engines Ltd., 26
Britannia Spring and Engineering Co., 160, 165
British Light Steel Pressings, 9
Burton Engineering Ltd., 146, 165
Butcher, Johnny, 107
buying, 171–7

C.K.D.s see kits (C.K.D.)
Caine, Alec, 34–40, 46–53, 55, 57, 67, 73, 89
California Association of Tiger Owners, 193
camshafts: technical specification, 244; tuning kits, 145–8
carburation: technical specification, 246–8; tuning kits, 150–56
Carmichael, Dan, 136

Carrozia Superleggera Touring Milano see Superleggera Touring Milano
chassis: numbers, 228–30; pitfalls, 171–2
Chrysler Corp., 68–70, 75
Chrysler (UK) Ltd., 180, 182–3
Chrysler V8 engine, 92
Clement Talbot, 9
clubs, 178–95
clutch: technical specification, 249; tuning kits, 157
Coad, Dennis, 166
Coftner, Al, 136
Cole, George, 107
Coleman, Peter, 29, 132
Commer, 8
competition, 94–140
connecting rod, 244–5
cooling system, 143, 159, 248
corrosion, 171–7
crankshaft, 244
Crompton, Jeff, 20
cylinders: technical specification, 243; tuning kits, 148–9

Danville Virginia National Races, 1965 136
Daytona 24-hour race, 1966, 136
Derrington, V.W., Ltd., 164
Devonshire House, 8
distributors, 149–50
Dixon, Freddie, Challenge Trophy, 132
Drolet, Miss, 136

Edwards, Mr (British Aerospace), 53
Elliot, Ray, 29
engine: numbers, 228–30; pitfalls when buying, 175–7; stabilizers, 158; tuning kits, 142–9
Evans, Frederick, 132
Eyre-Maunsell, Charles, 97–9

Fisher, Craig, 166
flywheel, 156–7

Ford Motor Co., 19
Ford V8 engine, 92
Fraser, Alan, 94, 95, 96
Fraser, Alan, Racing Team, 94, 131
French, Peter, 88
fuel pump, 248

Garrard, Norman, 41–2, 99, 101, 107, 111, 116
gearboxes: pitfalls when buying, 176–7; technical specification, 249
Girling, 39
Grand Prix D'Endurance, Riverside LA, 114–16
Green, Ted, 20
gudgeon pin, 245

Hadden, Arthur, 29, 34
Harper, Peter, 103–105, 107–12, 118–23, 127–31
Harrington 'A', 'B', 'C' and 'D' Type Alpine, 77–88
Harrington, Clifford, 76–78
Harrington Le Mans, 107; performance figures, 237
Harrington, Thomas, Ltd., 76–88
Hart, Ian, 166
Hartwell, George, Ltd., 79
Hillier, Bill, 29
Hillman Car Co., 8
Hillman Husky, 25
Hillman Minx, 9
Hillman Wizard, 9
Holroyd, John, 157
Hopkirk, Paddy, 103–105, 107–12, 127–31
Horrocks, Les, 54
Howe, Jeff, Exhausts and Cams Ltd., 146, 156, 165
Howes, Kenneth, 13–24
Humber Ltd., 8
Humber Sceptre, 88–92
Hunt, Gilbert, 75
hybrids, 76–92

ignition system, 248–9
International Circuit of Ireland: 1960, 97–9; 1961, 99
International Scottish Rally, 1961, 105–107

Jensen, 92
Johnson, Jeff, 36–7
Johnson, Johnny, 23, 34
Jopp, Peter, 103–105, 107–12, 127–31
Jordan, Dave, 123–5

Karrier Motors, 9
kits (C.K.D.), 89: chassis numbers, 229; production, 230
Kneeland, Bill, 123–5
Knight, Bill, 107

Le Mans: 1961, 107–12; 1962, 127–31; 1963, 131–2
Leigh, Ted, 27
Lewis, Tiny, 132
Lockheed, 39
Loewry Organization, 19
Loewry, Raymond, 14–16
Love, George, 68
lubrication, 248

McMillen, E. T., 99
Melvin, John, 105–106
Microcell Ltd., 54–7
Miles, Ken, 118–23
Minett, Irving, 68
Mitchell, Robert C., 68
Monte Carlo Rally 1960, 97
Moss, Stirling, 114–16

New Zealand Sunbeam Owners Club, 187–8

oil coolers, 143, 159
overdrive, 177

Pacific Tiger Club, 194–5
Panama Grand Prix, 1964, 136
Panks, John, 20
performance, 47, 55, 64–7, 70, 144, 231–7
Pickford Axle Exchange, 166
Piper Engineering, 146
pistons: clearances, 142, 145; technical specification, 245–6
Pountain, Keith, 88, 92
Price, Shenley, 94
Proctor, Peter, 103–105, 107–12, 118–23, 127–31

production figures, 230
propeller shaft, 250

Quality Springs Ltd., 165

Reed, Michael, 134
Road Development Engineers, 'Set 'em
  alight boys', 28–9
road tests, 47, 197–228
Robins-Day Ltd., 88
Rootes (Canada), 166
Rootes Competition Department, 99
Rootes, Geoffrey, 2nd Baron Rootes,
  20, 71, 75
Rootes Group: Chrysler take-over, 75;
  finances, 62; first links with Chrysler,
  68–70; origins, 7; strikes at Acton,
  54–9
Rootes Italia, 89
Rootes, Sir Reginald, 7, 20, 23, 68, 71,
  75
Rootes, Timothy, 42
Rootes, William, 7
Rootes, William Edward, 1st Baron
  Rootes, 7, 11, 23, 57, 68–71
Royal Automobile Club Rally, 1959,
  94–6
Royal Scottish Automobile Club *see*
  International Scottish Rally

Scott, Brian, 166
Sebring 12-hour race: 1961, 101–105;
  1962, 118–23; 1963, 123–5
Sesslar, Don, 134
Sheppard, Joe, 118–23
shock absorbers, 160–62
Singer Motors Ltd, 7
Smith, Rosemary, 136
Solex Carburettors, 63, 72, 154
spares, 178–95
Spencer, Gerry, 107
Sperling, Maurice, 29
Sports Car Club of America (SCCA)
  Championship: 1961, 112; 1964, 134
Sports Car (points) Championship
  Trophy, 99
springs, 160–62
steering: pitfalls when buying, 176;
  technical specification, 251
Stromberg Carburettors, 72, 154

Studebaker Motor Company, 19
SU Carburettors, 155–6
Sunbeam Alpine, press reviews, 42
Sunbeam Alpine Series 1:
  body dimensions, weights and
    capacities, 238–9
  carburation, 246
  chassis/floorpan, 25, 30
  chassis number, 229
  christening, 24
  disc brakes, 35–9
  flexing, 30–31
  mock up, 23, 32
  models, 20–22
  performance, 231–2
  production figures, 230
  prototypes, 25–38
  release, 11, 39–41
  road test, 197–205
Sunbeam Alpine Series 2:
  body dimensions, weights and
    capacities, 238–9
  carburation, 247
  chassis number, 229
  engine, 48
  introduction, 48
  performance, 233
  production figures, 230
  seats, 53
  special tuning log, 166–70
  Superleggera designs, 46–7, 49, 51–3
  tuning kits, 141
Sunbeam Alpine Series 3:
  adjustable steering, 54, 55
  body dimensions, weights and
    capacities, 239–40
  carburation, 63, 247
  chassis number, 229
  disc brakes, 60–62
  exhaust manifold, 62
  GT model, 55
  introduction, 60–62
  pedals, 57, 59
  performance, 234
  production, 62
  production figures, 230
  road test, 213–17
  seat design, 54–7
  Superleggera modifications, 62–3
  suspension, 60

255

Sunbeam Alpine Series 4:
    automatic transmission, 64–6
    body dimensions, weights and
        capacities, 240–41
    carburation, 247
    chassis number, 229
    engine design, 70
    introduction, 63–4
    performance, 235
    production figures, 230
    road test, 217–21
    synchromesh, 67
    trailing edges, 67
Sunbeam Alpine Series 5:
    alternator, 72
    announced, 72
    body dimensions, weights and
        capacities, 240–41
    carburation, 72, 248
    chassis number, 229
    performance, 70–71, 236
    production ceases, 75
    production figures, 230
    road test, 222–8
Sunbeam Alpine Club, 191–2
Sunbeam Alpine Owners Club (SAOC),
    88–9, 171, 178–85
Sunbeam Club of America, 190–91
Sunbeam Harrington Alpine *see*
    Harrington 'A' type Alpine
Sunbeam Harrington Le Mans, 79; road
    test, 205–213
Sunbeam Le Mans GT, 79
Sunbeam Motor Co., 9
Sunbeam Owners Association, 190
Sunbeam Owners Club of Sweden,
    189–90
Sunbeam Rapier, 25
Sunbeam Sports Car Club of South
    Africa, 188–9

Sunbeam Sports Car Owners Club of
    Canada, 186–7
Sunbeam and Talbot Owners Club, 186
Sunbeam Tiger Owners Club, 185–6
Sunbeam Tiger Owners Pacific, 193–4
Sunbeam Venezia, 88–92
Superleggera Touring Milano, 46, 49, 51,
    53, 59, 62–4, 89, 92
suspension: pitfalls when buying, 176;
    technical specification, 250–51; tuning
    kits, 144, 160–62

Tamburo, 103–105
Tarbun, Don, 29, 34
Targa hard top, 73
technical specifications, 243–52
Theodoli, Filippo, 118–25
Thoroughbred and Classic Car events,
    180, 182
Titus, Jerry, 123–5
torque loading figures, 251–2
Town and Country Motoring Festival
    1978, 182
Townsend, Lynn A, 68
tuning, special, 142–70

Unett, Bernard, 29, 53, 132, 134

valves, 243–4

Walden, Dennis, 29
Walton, Jack, 107
Ware, Peter, 36, 53–4
Warren, Lovis B., 68
Weber carburettors, 154–5
White, Ted, 20
Winter, Bernard, 20, 23
Wright, Dick, 107

Zenith carburettors, 63, 150–53